A Pen Warmed-up in Hell

A PEN WARMED-UP IN HELL

Mark Twain in Protest

edited by
Frederick Anderson

PERENNIAL LIBRARY
HARPER & ROW, PUBLISHERS
New York, Evanston, San Francisco, London

A hardcover edition of this book is available from Harper & Row, Publishers, Inc.

A PEN WARMED-UP IN HELL:
MARK TWAIN IN PROTEST

 For information address Harper & Row, Publishers, Inc., 10 East 53d Street, New York, N.Y. 10022. Published simultaneously in Canada by Fitzhenry & Whiteside Limited, Toronto.

First PERENNIAL LIBRARY edition published 1973
STANDARD BOOK NUMBER: 06-080279-0

3-73

"Battle Hymn of the Republic (Brought Down to Date)" from *Mark Twain: Social Critic*. Copyright © 1958 by Mark Twain Company. Published by International Publishers.

"A Salutation-Speech" originally appeared in *The New York Herald.*

"The Private History of a Campaign That Failed" from *The American Claimant and Other Stories and Sketches*. Published by Harper & Row, Publishers, Inc.

"As Regards Patriotism"; "To the Person Sitting in Darkness"; "The War-Prayer"; "Bible Teaching and Religious Practice"; "The United States of Lyncherdom," and "The Dervish and the Offensive Stranger" from *Europe and Elsewhere*. Published by Harper & Row, Publishers, Inc.

Passage from "Glances at History (Suppressed)"; Extract from an article in " 'The Radical,' January 916"; and "The Lowest Animal (prefatory note)" from *Letters From the Earth*. Published by Harper & Row, Publishers, Inc.

"History of War and Dishonorable War" from *Mark Twain's Mysterious Stranger Manuscripts,* edited with an Introduction by William M. Gibson. © 1969 by The Mark Twain Company. Originally published by the University of California Press; reprinted by permission of The Regents of the University of California.

"Letter to Sylvester Baxter" from *Mark Twain's Letters*. Published by Harper & Row, Publishers, Inc.

"Letter to William T. Stead" from *Mark Twain's Letters*. Published by Harper & Row, Publishers, Inc.

"Grief and Mourning for the Night" from *Mark Twain's Autobiography*. Published by Harper & Row, Publishers, Inc.

"The Great Revolution in Pitcairn" originally appeared in the *Atlantic Monthly*.

"A True Story, Repeated Word for Word as I Heard It" from *Sketches New and Old*. Published by Harper & Row, Publishers, Inc.

"About Smells" and "Goldsmith's Friend Abroad Again" originally appeared in *Galaxy*.

"A River Village and a Lynch Mob" from *The Adventures of Huckleberry Finn*. Published by Harper & Row, Publishers, Inc.

"The Whole Human Race" from *Mark Twain in Eruption.* Published by Harper & Row, Publishers, Inc.

Contents

The Human Condition

Introduction

When Mark Twain completed *A Connecticut Yankee* he wrote to William Dean Howells in 1889 of his frustration at not having been able to say all that he believed:

> Well, my book is written—let it go. But if it were only to write over again there wouldn't be so many things left out. They burn in me; and they keep multiplying and multiplying; but now they can't ever be said. And besides, they would require a library—and a pen warmed-up in hell.

He warmed his pen often in the twenty years that remained of his life and the views he expressed ranged as widely as public affairs and private rage demanded. He can be quoted by people of almost any political persuasion for he expressed views as contradictory as his own character was inconsistent. What it is most important to remember is that he was not a subscriber to any systematic belief, that in fact he was most fervent in his defense of the right of all men to contrary opinions. The issue rather than a doctrine determined a man's responsibility.

During the 1884 Presidential contest between two unsavory candidates, Cleveland and Blaine, he argued the question of party loyalty and private conviction with Howells:

> Somehow I can't seem to rest quiet under the idea of your voting for Blaine. I believe you said something about the country and the party. Certainly allegiance to these is well; but as certainly a man's first duty is to his own conscience and honor—the party and the country come second to that, and never first. I don't ask you to vote *at all*—I only urge you to not soil yourself by voting for Blaine. . . . It is not necessary to vote for Cleveland; the only necessary thing to do, as I understand it, is that a man shall keep *himself* clean (by withholding his vote for an improper man), even though the party and the country go to destruction in consequence.

Mark Twain's various responses to social evil could encompass retreat from decision when insupportable choices were offered, a plea for modification of an existing system by reform, and demand for revolution when reform no longer seemed possible. The one constant was his insistence on the right to the exercise of independent choice and the injustice of imposing the views of one group or person upon another. In an address ironically titled "Consistency," defending the Mugwumps who had bolted from the Republican party in 1884, he elaborately developed the right to changing and independent views:

> This infamous doctrine of allegiance to party plays directly into the hands of politicians of the baser sort—and doubtless for that it was borrowed—or stolen—from the monarchical system. It enables them to foist upon the country officials whom no self-respecting man would vote for, if he could but come to understand that loyalty

to himself is his first and highest duty, not loyalty to any party name. The wire-workers, convention-packers know they are not obliged to put up the fittest man for the office, for they know that the docile party will vote for any forkèd thing they put up, even though it do not even strictly resemble a man. . . . This is a funny business, all round. The same men who enthusiastically preach loyal consistency to church and party, are always ready and willing and anxious to persuade a Chinaman or an Indian or a Kanaka to desert his Church, or a fellow-American to desert his party. The man who deserts to them is all that is high and pure and beautiful—apparently; the man who deserts from them is all that is foul and despicable. . . . Loyalty to petrified opinions never yet broke a chain or freed a human soul in this world—and never will.

The dual effect when the self-righteous impose their principles and practice upon others was a subject to which he would return. Even more than it is an indictment of military aggression, "The War-Prayer" is an ironic description of the limited view of petitioners who, when invoking success for their cause, fail to recognize the corollary disasters they are beseeching for their enemies. This double vision in which injustice is seen as the inevitable companion of a desirable goal is also the basis for the dialogue between "The Dervish and the Offensive Stranger" where he describes the devastation inflicted upon the American Indian by intruders who would settle and "civilize" the Indians' lands.

Injustice wherever it might be found was the object of his wrath although his attacks were sometimes ingenuous and his courage to express his convictions vacillated. Although aware of his influence as a public figure, Mark Twain recognized private responsibilities to himself and those around him. Consequently his attitude toward published expression of unpopular views was ambivalent. His own feelings were often involved or contradictory, moreover, and his instincts for comfort and approval were large. The result of this conflict of impulses as often as not allowed prudence to take precedence over principle.

Mark Twain recognized the discrepancy between theory and practice and acknowledged a distinction between his "*real* opinions" and his "*published* opinions." Of course he transgressed his rule against expression of private views in public print when "the inclination to do it was stronger than my diplomatic instincts, and I had to obey and take the consequences." He explained the decision to take the consequences as a convoluted form of self-indulgence. "We never do *any* duty for the duty's sake but only for the mere personal satisfaction we get out of doing that duty." On an occasion when he decided against assuming the consequences of his duty he said that to do so "would damn me before my time and I didn't want to be useful to the world on such expensive conditions."

The limitations of Mark Twain's sense of history, an understanding of men rather than issues, further restricted his conception of social responsibility. His role as a critic of political and economic injustice appears to have been one thrust upon him by observation of wrong rather than one which emerged from a conviction of right. His statements on the individual's need to "preserve a clean vote"—by not voting

—is clearly that of a passive rejection of evil rather than a positive belief in the function of working for change. He repeatedly said that although he could see change was needed he was not the man to bring it about. Hank Morgan, Mark Twain's spokesman in *A Connecticut Yankee,* regards with disgust the debased condition of a state ruled by hereditary aristocracy and concludes that only revolution will establish the rights of man. He believes that "all revolutions that will succeed, must *begin* in blood . . . and I was the wrong man for them." As such Mark Twain must be recognized as a reluctant radical, an amateur reformer. His advice for amelioration often was to withdraw rather than counterattack: "It is easier to stay out than get out" is one of the maxims he created for "Pudd'nhead Wilson's New Calendar." In the same sequence of maxims he recorded a view of public responsibility: "It is by the goodness of God that in our country we have those three unspeakably precious things: freedom of speech, freedom of conscience, and the prudence never to practice either of them." That prudence he attributed to what he called "corn-pone opinions":

> The . . . idea was that a man is not independent, and cannot afford views which might interfere with his bread and butter. If he would prosper, he must train with the majority; in matters of large moment, like politics and religion, he must think and feel with the bulk of his neighbors or suffer damage in his social standing and in his business prosperities. He must restrict himself to corn-pone opinions—at least on the surface. He must get his opinions from other people; he must reason out none for himself; he must have no first-hand views.

In 1906 he recalled an episode when the San Francisco newspaper for which he was a reporter forty years before had suppressed his indignant account of "some hoodlums chasing and stoning a Chinaman who was heavily laden with the weekly wash of his Christian customers" while a policeman watched "with an amused interest." The paper, he was told, catered to the poor and could not afford to offend its readers. "The Irish were the poor . . . and they hated the Chinamen."

I felt a deep shame in being situated as I was—slave of such a journal as the *Morning Call*. If I had been still loftier I would have thrown up my berth and gone out and starved, like any other hero. But I had never had any experience. I had *dreamed* heroism, like everybody, but I had no practice and I didn't know how to begin. I couldn't bear to begin with starving. I had already come near to that once or twice in my life, and got no real enjoyment out of remembering about it. I knew I couldn't get another berth if I resigned. I knew it perfectly well. Therefore I swallowed my humiliation and stayed where I was.

Although he would become a forthright exponent of racial and economic justice, the influences of his early years were not promising.

In my schoolboy days I had no aversion to slavery. I was not aware that there was anything wrong about it. No one arraigned it in my hearing; the local papers said nothing against it; the local pulpit taught us that God approved it, that it was a holy thing, and that the doubter need only look in the Bible if he wished to settle his mind—and then the texts were read aloud to us to make the matter sure; if the slaves themselves had any aversion to slavery, they were wise and said nothing. In Hannibal we seldom saw a slave misused; on the farm, never.

Even in *Pudd'nhead Wilson,* his most sustained and conscious effort to deal with slavery and the moral stupor which that institution imposed upon the society of which it was a part, it is impossible to ignore his confusion. The views which emerge from the tangled themes of his novel are elusive and contradictory. To what extent does Mark Twain identify physical, cultural, and moral inferiority with the effect of racial heredity and to what extent is it a product of cultural training? The narrative has so effectively interinvolved both influences on the development of each character that the only reasonably certain conclusion is that slavery as a total evil has totally corrupted all of the participating parties. Although the reader's sympathies may be engaged by several of the characters, only the untainted Northerner, David Wilson, is able to surmount the evils, implicit and expressed, which engross the members of the community of Dawson's Landing.

But in his conscious and reasoned views expressed about minorities, Mark Twain's principles are clear if somewhat romanticized. He wrote Albert Sonnichsen, author of *Ten Months a Captive Among the Filipinos,* in 1901:

We all take a high pleasure in seeing our theories vindicated and supported. One of my theories is, that the hearts of men are about alike, all over the world, no matter what their skin-complexions may be. Another notion of mine is that civilizations proceed from the heart rather than from the head, and that wherever one finds a nation whose hearts are not debauched, the civilization that obtains in that nation is high, and its possessors may be trusted to be able to govern themselves about as well as we . . . could do it for them. Your book goes far to persuade me that the infusion of bastard and un-American civilization which we have injected into the Filipino has been a good deal of a damage to him.

A thriving capacity for intellectual growth and recurrent if inconstant self-analysis made him aware of his progress from the assumptions of a backwoods Southern village to the convictions of an exponent of international revolution by 1887 when he wrote to Howells:

> How stunning are the changes which age makes in a man while he sleeps. When I finished Carlyle's French Revolution in 1871, I was a Girondin; every time I have read it since, I have read it differently—being influenced and changed, little by little, by life and environment (and Taine, and St. Simon): and now I lay the book down once more, and recognize that I am a Sansculotte! —And not a pale, characterless Sansculotte, but a Marat. Carlyle teaches no such gospel: so the change is in *me* —in my vision of the evidences.

As the distance from the frontier increased, his concerns moved from domestic issues to international affairs until these became almost an obsession during the last decade of his life which was also the first decade of this century. America's recurrent intervention in the concerns of other nations was at one of its periodic peaks as Mark Twain, whose literary career was essentially completed, addressed his final years to serving as critic at large of the principle of Manifest Destiny.

After nearly ten years' residence abroad including a lecture tour around the world he was interviewed by a London correspondent for the New York *World* on 6 October 1900. Although unfamiliar with American reaction to the United States' involvement in China and the Philippines, he was certain of his own:

You ask me about what is called imperialism. Well, I have formed views about that question. I am at the disadvantage of not knowing whether our people are for or against spreading themselves over the face of the globe. I should be sorry if they are, for I don't think that it is wise or a necessary development. As to China, I quite approve of our Government's action in getting free of that complication. They are withdrawing, I understand, having done what they wanted. That is quite right. We have no more business in China than in any other country that is not ours. There is the case of the Philippines. I have tried hard, and yet I cannot for the life of me comprehend how we got into that mess. Perhaps we could not have avoided it—perhaps it was inevitable that we should come to be fighting the natives of those islands—but I cannot understand it, and have never been able to get at the bottom of the origin of our antagonism to the natives. I thought we should act as their protector—not try to get them under our heel. We were to relieve them from Spanish tyranny to enable them to set up a government of their own, and we were to stand by and see that it got a fair trial. It was not to be a government according to our ideas, but a government that represented the feeling of the majority of the Filipinos, a government according to Filipino ideas. That would have been a worthy mission for the United States. But now—why, we have got into a mess, a quagmire from which each fresh step renders the difficulty of extrication immensely greater. I'm sure I wish I could see what we were getting out of it, and all it means to us as a nation.

A few days later, upon his arrival in the United States, for an interview published in the New York *Herald* on 16 October 1900, he described the evolution of his thought during the preceding four years:

I left these shores, at Vancouver, a red-hot imperialist. I wanted the American eagle to go screaming into the Pacific. It seemed tiresome and tame for it to content itself with the Rockies. Why not spread its wings over the Philippines, I asked myself? And I thought it would be a real good thing to do.

I said to myself, Here are a people who have suffered for three centuries. We can make them as free as ourselves, give them a government and country of their own, put a miniature of the American constitution afloat in the Pacific, start a brand new republic to take its place among the free nations of the world. It seemed to me a great task to which we had addressed ourselves.

But I have thought some more, since then, and I have read carefully the treaty of Paris, and I have seen that we do not intend to free, but to subjugate the people of the Philippines. We have gone there to conquer, not to redeem.

We have also pledged the power of this country to maintain and protect the system established in the Philippines by the Friars.

It should, it seems to me, be our pleasure and duty to make those people free, and let them deal with their own domestic questions in their own way. And so I am an anti-imperialist. I am opposed to having the eagle put its talons on any other land.

Imperialistic wars were indefensible but Mark Twain defended, demanded, wars of revolution to free the oppressed from despotic rulers and unresponsive governments. He fervently endorsed the Russo-Japanese conflict as a means for the overthrow of the Czarist regime and deplored its peaceful resolution by the Treaty of Portsmouth. In the Boston *Globe* of 30 August 1905 he commented:

> Russia was on the high road to emancipation from an insane and intolerable slavery; I was hoping there would be no peace until Russian liberty was safe. I think that this was a holy war in the best and noblest sense of that abused term, and that no war was ever charged with a higher mission; I think there can be no doubt that that mission is now defeated and Russia's chains re-riveted, this time to stay. I think the Czar will now withdraw the small humanities that have been forced from him and resume his medieval barbarisms with a relieved spirit and an immeasurable joy. I think Russian liberty has had its last chance, and has lost it. I think nothing has been gained by the peace that is remotely comparable to what has been sacrificed by it. One more battle would have abolished the waiting chains of billions upon billions of unborn Russians, and I wish it could have been fought. I hope I am mistaken, yet in all sincerity I believe that this peace is entitled to rank as the most conspicuous disaster in political history.

Rage and righteousness often carried his prose to admirable extremes of ferocious vituperation or icy irony, but sometimes it entrapped him in shrill and wandering argument. His well-justified effort to expose the incredible cruelties inflicted at King Leopold's direction upon the native population of the Congo Free State was diffuse and, now the issues are resolved, tedious. This pamphlet of more than forty printed pages collects an unwieldy mass of newspaper clippings and quotations from a variety of other sources which are tacked together with bits of rather perfunctory attempts at irony. So much of the lengthy piece consists of ephemeral accounts of isolated charges now obscure to all except a specialized historian that its contemporary interest is negligible.

But much more of what he wrote concerns wrongs evidently inescapable in contemporary society. His bitterness about the terrors imposed by useless war, the squalor of racial injustice, the fraudulent distribution of wealth, and the exploitation of their citizens by indifferent governments could have been aroused by any issue of a current newspaper. People many generations removed from his own can share Mark Twain's perception of evil, feelings of guilt, and expressions of rage at the world's injustices. Although he made it seventy years ago, his readers today can readily recognize the conditions which elicited his proposal: "Let us abolish policemen who carry clubs and revolvers, and put in a squad of poets armed to the teeth with poems on Spring and Love."

On War

I bring you the stately matron named Christendom, returning bedraggled, besmirched and dishonored from pirate-raids in Kiao-Chow, Manchuria, South Africa and the Philippines, with her soul full of meanness, her pocket full of boodle and her mouth full of pious hypocrisies. Give her soap and a towel, but hide the looking-glass.

—"*A salutation-speech from the Nineteenth Century to the Twentieth, taken down in short-hand by Mark Twain*" (*December 31, 1900*)

Battle Hymn of the Republic
(Brought Down to Date)
(1900?)

Mine eyes have seen the orgy of the launching of the
Sword;
He is searching out the hoardings where the stranger's wealth is stored;
He hath loosed his fateful lightnings, and with woe
and death has scored;
His lust is marching on.

I have seen him in the watch-fires of a hundred
circling camps,
They have builded him an altar in the Eastern dews
and damps;
I have read his doomful mission by the dim and
flaring lamps—
His night is marching on.

I have read his bandit gospel writ in burnished rows
of steel:
"As ye deal with my pretensions, so with you my
wrath shall deal;
Let the faithless son of Freedom crush the patriot
with his heel;
Lo, Greed is marching on!"

We have legalized the strumpet and are guarding her
retreat;*

* In Manila the Government has placed a certain industry under the protection of our flag. (M.T.)

Greed is seeking out commercial souls before his
judgment seat;
O, be swift, ye clods, to answer him! be jubilant my
feet!
Our god is marching on!

In a sordid slime harmonious, Greed was born in
yonder ditch,
With a longing in his bosom—and for others' goods
an itch—
As Christ died to make men holy, let men die to
make us rich—
Our god is marching on.

The Private History of a Campaign That Failed
(1885)

You have heard from a great many people who did something in the war; is it not fair and right that you listen a little moment to one who started out to do something in it, but didn't? Thousands entered the war, got just a taste of it, and then stepped out again, permanently. These, by their very numbers, are respectable, and are therefore entitled to a sort of voice,—not a loud one, but a modest one; not a boastful one, but an apologetic one. They ought not to be allowed much space among better people—people who did something—I grant that; but they ought at least to be allowed to state why they didn't do anything, and also to explain the process by which they didn't do anything. Surely this kind of light must have a sort of value.

Out West there was a good deal of confusion in men's minds during the first months of the great trouble—a good deal of unsettledness, of leaning first this way, then that, then the other way. It was hard for us to get our bearings. I call to mind an instance of this. I was piloting on the Mississippi when the news came that South Carolina had gone out of the Union on the 20th of December, 1860. My pilot-mate was a New Yorker. He was strong for the Union; so was I. But he would not listen to me with any patience; my loyalty was smirched, to his eye, because my father had owned slaves. I said, in palliation of this dark fact, that I had heard my father say, some years before he died, that slavery was a great wrong, and that he would free the solitary negro he then owned if he could think it right to give away the property of the family when he was so straitened in means. My mate retorted that a mere impulse was nothing—anybody could pretend to a good impulse; and went on decrying my Unionism and libeling my ancestry. A month later the secession atmosphere had considerably thickened on the Lower Mississippi, and I became a rebel; so did he. We were together in New Orleans, the 26th of January, when Louisiana went out of the Union. He did his full share of the rebel shouting, but was bitterly opposed to letting me do mine. He said that I came of bad stock—of a father who had been willing to set slaves free. In the following summer he was piloting a Federal gunboat and shouting for the Union again, and I was in the Confederate army. I held his note for some borrowed money. He was one of the most upright men I ever knew; but he repudiated that note without hesitation, because I was a rebel, and the son of a man who owned slaves.

In that summer—of 1861—the first wash of the wave of war broke upon the shores of Missouri. Our State was invaded by the Union forces. They took possession of St. Louis, Jefferson Barracks, and some other points. The Governor, Claib Jackson, issued his proclamation calling out fifty thousand militia to repel the invader.

I was visiting in the small town where my boyhood had been spent—Hannibal, Marion County. Several of us got together in a secret place by night and formed ourselves into a military company. One Tom Lyman, a young fellow of a good deal of spirit but of no military experience, was made captain; I was made second lieutenant. We had no first lieutenant; I do not know why; it was long ago. There were fifteen of us. By the advice of an innocent connected with the organization, we called ourselves the Marion Rangers. I do not remember that any one found fault with the name. I did not; I thought it sounded quite well. The young fellow who proposed this title was perhaps a fair sample of the kind of stuff we were made of. He was young, ignorant, good-natured, well-meaning, trivial, full of romance, and given to reading chivalric novels and singing forlorn love-ditties. He had some pathetic little nickel-plated aristocratic instincts, and detested his name, which was Dunlap; detested it, partly because it was nearly as common in that region as Smith, but mainly because it had a plebeian sound to his ear. So he tried to ennoble it by writing it in this way: *d'Unlap*. That contented his eye, but left his ear unsatisfied, for people gave the new name the same old pronunciation—emphasis on the front end of it. He then did the bravest thing that can be imagined,—a thing to make one shiver when one remembers how the world is given to resenting shams and affectations; he began to write his name so: *d'Un Lap*. And he waited patiently through the long storm of mud that was flung at this work of art, and he had his reward at last; for he lived to see that name accepted, and the emphasis put where he wanted it, by people who had known him all his life, and to whom the tribe of Dunlaps had been as familiar as the rain and the sunshine for forty years. So sure of victory at last is the courage that can wait. He said he had found, by consulting some ancient French chronicles, that the name was rightly and originally written d'Un Lap; and said that if it were translated into English it would mean Peterson: *Lap*, Latin or Greek, he said, for stone or rock, same as the French *pierre*, that is to say, Peter; *d'*, of or from; *un*, a or one; hence, d'Un Lap, of or from a stone or a Peter; that is to say, one who is the son of a stone, the son of a Peter—Peterson. Our militia company were not learned, and the explanation confused them; so they called him Peterson Dunlap. He proved useful to us in his way; he named our camps for us, and he generally struck a name that was "no slouch," as the boys said.

That is one sample of us. Another was Ed Stevens, son of the town jeweler,—trim-built, handsome, graceful, neat as a cat; bright, educated, but given over entirely to fun. There was nothing serious in life to him. As far as he was concerned, this military expedition of ours was simply a holiday. I should say that about half of us looked upon it in the same way; not consciously, perhaps, but unconsciously. We did not think; we were not capable of it. As for myself, I was full of unreasoning joy to be done with turning out of bed at midnight and four in the morning, for a while; grateful to have a change, new scenes, new occupations, a new interest. In my thoughts that was as far as I went; I did not go into the details; as a rule one doesn't at twenty-four.

Another sample was Smith, the blacksmith's apprentice. This vast donkey had some pluck, of a slow and sluggish nature, but a soft heart; at one time he would knock a horse down for some impropriety, and at another he would get homesick and cry. However, he had one ultimate credit to his account which some of us hadn't: he stuck to the war, and was killed in battle at last.

Jo Bowers, another sample, was a huge, good-natured, flax-headed lubber; lazy, sentimental, full of harmless brag, a grumbler by nature; an experienced, industrious, ambitious, and often quite picturesque liar, and yet not a successful one, for he had had no intelligent training, but was allowed to come up just any way. This life was serious enough to him, and seldom satisfactory. But he was a good fellow anyway, and the boys all liked him. He was made orderly sergeant; Stevens was made corporal.

These samples will answer—and they are quite fair ones. Well, this herd of cattle started for the war. What could you expect of them? They did as well as they knew how, but really what was justly to be expected of them? Nothing, I should say. That is what they did.

We waited for a dark night, for caution and secrecy were necessary; then, toward midnight, we stole in couples and from various directions to the Griffith place, beyond the town; from that point we set out together on foot. Hannibal lies at the extreme southeastern corner of Marion County, on the Mississippi River; our objective point was the hamlet of New London, ten miles away, in Ralls County.

The first hour was all fun, all idle nonsense and laughter. But that could not be kept up. The steady trudging came to be like work; the play had somehow oozed out of it; the stillness of the woods and the somberness of the night began to throw a depressing influence over the spirits of the boys, and presently the talking died out and each person shut himself up in his own thoughts. During the last half of the second hour nobody said a word.

Now we approached a log farm-house where, according to report, there was a guard of five Union soldiers. Lyman called a halt; and there, in the deep gloom of the overhanging branches, he began to whisper a plan of assault upon that house, which made the gloom more depressing than it was before. It was a crucial moment; we realized, with a cold suddenness, that here was no jest—we were standing face to face with actual war. We were equal to the occasion. In our response there was no hesitation, no indecision: we said that if Lyman wanted to meddle with those soldiers, he could go ahead and do it; but if he waited for us to follow him, he would wait a long time.

Lyman urged, pleaded, tried to shame us, but it had no effect. Our course was plain, our minds were made up: we would flank the farm-house—go out around. And that is what we did.

We struck into the woods and entered upon a rough time, stumbling over roots, getting tangled in vines, and torn by briers. At last we reached an open place in a safe region, and sat down, blown and hot, to cool off and nurse our scratches and bruises. Lyman was annoyed, but the rest of us were cheerful; we had flanked the farm-house, we had made our first military movement, and it was a success; we had nothing to fret about, we were feeling just the other way. Horse-play and laughing began again; the expedition was become a holiday frolic once more.

Then we had two more hours of dull trudging and ultimate silence and depression; then, about dawn, we straggled into New London, soiled, heel-blistered, fagged with our little march, and all of us except Stevens in a sour and raspy humor and privately down on the war. We stacked our shabby old shotguns in Colonel Ralls's barn, and then went in a body and breakfasted with that veteran of the Mexican war. Afterwards he took us to a distant meadow, and there in the shade of a tree we listened to an old-fashioned speech from him, full of gunpowder and glory, full of that adjective-piling, mixed metaphor, and windy declamation which was regarded as eloquence in that ancient time and that remote region; and then he swore us on the Bible to be faithful to the State of Missouri and drive all invaders from her soil, no matter whence they might come or under what flag they might march. This mixed us considerably, and we could not make out just what service we were embarked in; but Colonel Ralls, the practiced politician and phrase-juggler, was not similarly in doubt; he knew quite clearly that he had invested us in the cause of the Southern Confederacy. He closed the solemnities by belting around me the sword which his neighbor, Colonel Brown, had worn at Buena Vista and Molino del Rey; and he accompanied this act with another impressive blast.

Then we formed in line of battle and marched four

miles to a shady and pleasant piece of woods on the border of the far-reaching expanses of a flowery prairie. It was an enchanting region for war—our kind of war.

We pierced the forest about half a mile, and took up a strong position, with some low, rocky, and wooded hills behind us, and a purling, limpid creek in front. Straightway half the command were in swimming, and the other half fishing. The ass with the French name gave this position a romantic title, but it was too long, so the boys shortened and simplified it to Camp Ralls.

We occupied an old maple-sugar camp, whose half-rotted troughs were still propped against the trees. A long corn-crib served for sleeping quarters for the battalion. On our left, half a mile away, was Mason's farm and house; and he was a friend to the cause. Shortly after noon the farmers began to arrive from several directions, with mules and horses for our use, and these they lent us for as long as the war might last, which they judged would be about three months. The animals were of all sizes, all colors, and all breeds. They were mainly young and frisky, and nobody in the command could stay on them long at a time; for we were town boys, and ignorant of horsemanship. The creature that fell to my share was a very small mule, and yet so quick and active that it could throw me without difficulty; and it did this whenever I got on it. Then it would bray—stretching its neck out, laying its ears back, and spreading its jaws till you could see down to its works. It was a disagreeable animal, in every way. If I took it by the bridle and tried to lead it off the grounds, it would sit down and brace back, and no one could budge it. However, I was not entirely destitute of military resources, and I did presently manage to spoil this game; for I had seen many a steamboat aground in my time, and knew a trick or two which even a grounded mule would be obliged to respect. There was a well by the corn-crib; so I substituted thirty fathom of rope for the bridle, and fetched him home with the windlass.

I will anticipate here sufficiently to say that we did learn to ride, after some days' practice, but never well. We could not learn to like our animals; they were not choice ones, and most of them had annoying peculiarities of one kind or another. Stevens's horse would carry him, when he was not noticing, under the huge excrescences which form on the trunks of oak-trees and wipe him out of the saddle; in this way Stevens got several bad hurts. Sergeant Bowers's horse was very large and tall, with slim, long legs, and looked like a railroad bridge. His size enabled him to reach all about, and as far as he wanted to, with his head; so he was always biting Bowers's legs. On the march, in the sun, Bowers slept a good deal; and as soon as the horse recognized that he was asleep he would reach around and bite him on the leg. His legs were black and blue with bites. This was the only thing that could ever make him swear, but this always did; whenever the horse bit him he always swore, and of course Stevens, who laughed at everything, laughed at this, and would even get into such convulsions over it as to lose his balance and fall off his horse; and then Bowers, already irritated by the pain of the horse-bite, would resent the laughter with hard language, and there would be a quarrel; so that horse made no end of trouble and bad blood in the command.

However, I will get back to where I was—our first afternoon in the sugar-camp. The sugar-troughs came very handy as horse-troughs, and we had plenty of corn to fill them with. I ordered Sergeant Bowers to feed my mule; but he said that if I reckoned he went to war to be dry-nurse to a mule, it wouldn't take me very long to find out my mistake. I believed that this was insubordination, but I was full of uncertanties about everything military, and so I let the thing pass, and went and ordered Smith, the blacksmith's apprentice, to feed the mule; but he merely gave me a large cold, sarcastic grin, such as an ostensibly seven-year-old horse gives you when you lift his lip and find he is fourteen, and turned his back on me. I then went to the captain, and asked if it was not right and proper and military for me to have an orderly. He said it was, but as there was only one orderly in the corps, it was but right that he himself should have Bowers on his staff. Bowers said he wouldn't serve on anybody's staff; and if anybody thought he could make him, let him try it. So, of course, the thing had to be dropped; there was no other way.

Next, nobody would cook; it was considered a degradation; so we had no dinner. We lazied the rest of the pleasant afternoon away, some dozing under the trees, some smoking cobpipes and talking sweethearts and war, some playing games. By late suppertime all hands were famished; and to meet the difficulty all hands turned to, on an equal footing, and gathered wood, built fires, and cooked the meal.

Afterward everything was smooth for a while; then trouble broke out between the corporal and the sergeant, each claiming to rank the other. Nobody knew which was the higher office; so Lyman had to settle the matter by making the rank of both officers equal. The commander of an ignorant crew like that has many troubles and vexations which probably do not occur in the regular army at all. However, with the song-singing and yarn-spinning around the camp-fire, everything presently became serene again; and by and by we raked the corn down level in one end of the crib, and all went to bed on it, tying a horse to the door, so that he would neigh if any one tried to get in.*

We had some horsemanship drill every forenoon; then, afternoons, we rode off here and there in squads a few miles, and visited the farmers' girls, and had a youthful good time, and got an honest good dinner or supper, and then home again to camp, happy and content.

For a time, life was idly delicious; it was perfect; there was nothing to mar it. Then came some farmers with an alarm one day. They said it was rumored

* It was always my impression that that was what the horse was there for, and I know that it was also the impression of at least one other of the command, for we talked about it at the time, and admired the military ingenuity of the device: but when I was out West three years ago I was told by Mr. A. G. Fuqua, a member of our company, that the horse was his, that the leaving him tied at the door was a matter of mere forgetfulness, and that to attribute it to intelligent invention was to give him quite too much credit. In support of his position, he called my attention to the suggestive fact that the artifice was not employed again. I had not thought of that before. (M.T.)

that the enemy were advancing in our direction, from over Hyde's prairie. The result was a sharp stir among us, and general consternation. It was a rude awakening from our pleasant trance. The rumor was but a rumor—nothing definite about it; so, in the confusion, we did not know which way to retreat. Lyman was for not retreating at all, in these uncertain circumstances; but he found that if he tried to maintain that attitude he would fare badly, for the command were in no humor to put up with insubordination. So he yielded the point and called a council of war—to consist of himself and the three other officers; but the privates made such a fuss about being left out, that we had to allow them to be present. I mean we had to allow them to remain, for they were already present, and doing the most of the talking too. The question was, which way to retreat; but all were so flurried that nobody seemed to have even a guess to offer. Except Lyman. He explained in a few calm words, that inasmuch as the enemy were approaching from over Hyde's prairie, our course was simple: all we had to do was not to retreat *toward* him; any other direction would answer our needs perfectly. Everybody saw in a moment how true this was, and how wise; so Lyman got a great many compliments. It was now decided that we should fall back on Mason's farm.

It was after dark by this time, and as we could not know how soon the enemy might arrive, it did not seem best to try to take the horses and things with us; so we only took the guns and ammunition, and started at once. The route was very rough and hilly and rocky, and presently the night grew very black and rain began to fall; so we had a troublesome time of it, struggling and stumbling along in the dark; and soon some person slipped and fell, and then the next person behind stumbled over him and fell, and so did the rest, one after the other; and then Bowers came with the keg of powder in his arms, whilst the command were all mixed together, arms and legs, on the muddy slope; and so he fell, of course, with the keg, and this started the whole detachment down the hill in a body, and they landed in the brook at the bottom in a pile, and each that was undermost pulling the hair and scratching and biting those that were on top of him; and those that were being scratched and bitten scratching and biting the rest in their turn, and all saying they would die before they would ever go to war again if they ever got out of this brook this time, and the invader might rot for all they cared, and the country along with him—and all such talk as that, which was dismal to hear and take part in, in such smothered, low voices, and such a grisly dark place and so wet, and the enemy may be coming any moment.

The keg of powder was lost, and the guns too; so the growling and complaining continued straight along whilst the brigade pawed around the pasty hillside and slopped around in the brook hunting for these things; consequently we lost considerable time at this; and then we heard a sound, and held our breath and listened, and it seemed to be the enemy coming, though it could have been a cow, for it had a cough like a cow; but we did not wait, but left a couple of guns behind and struck out for Mason's again as briskly as we could scramble along in the dark. But we got lost presently among the rugged little ravines, and wasted a deal of time finding the way again, so it was after nine when we reached Mason's stile at last; and then before we could open our mouths to give the countersign, several dogs came bounding over the fence, with great riot and noise, and each of them took a soldier by the slack of his trousers and began to back away with him. We could not shoot the dogs without endangering the persons they were attached to; so we had to look on, helpless, at what was perhaps the most mortifying spectacle of the Civil War. There was light enough, and to spare, for the Masons had now run out on the porch with candles in their hands. The old man and his son came and undid the dogs without difficulty, all but Bowers's; but they couldn't undo his dog, they didn't know his combination; he was of the bull kind, and seemed to be set with a Yale time-lock; but they got him loose at last with some scalding water, of which Bowers got his share and returned thanks. Peterson Dunlap afterwards made up a fine name for this engagement, and also for the night march which preceded it, but both have long ago faded out of my memory.

We now went into the house, and they began to ask us a world of questions, whereby it presently came out that we did not know anything concerning who or what we were running from; so the old gentleman made himself very frank, and said we were a curious breed of soldiers, and guessed we could be depended on to end up the war in time, because no government could stand the expense of the shoe-leather we should cost it trying to follow us around.

"Marion *Rangers!* good name, b'gosh!" said he. And wanted to know why we hadn't had a picket-guard at the place where the road entered the prairie, and why we hadn't sent out a scouting party to spy out the enemy and bring us an account of his strength, and so on, before jumping up and stampeding out of a strong position upon a mere vague rumor—and so on and so forth, till he made us all feel shabbier than the dogs had done, not half so enthusiastically welcome. So we went to bed shamed and low-spirited; except Stevens. Soon Stevens began to devise a garment for Bowers which could be made to automatically display his battle-scars to the grateful, or conceal them from the envious, according to his occasions; but Bowers was in no humor for this, so there was a fight, and when it was over Stevens had some battle-scars of his own to think about.

Then we got a little sleep. But after all we had gone through, our activities were not over for the night; for about two o'clock in the morning we heard a shout of warning from down the lane, accompanied by a chorus from all the dogs, and in a moment everybody was up and flying around to find out what the alarm was about. The alarmist was a horseman who gave notice that a detachment of Union soldiers was on its way from Hannibal with orders to capture and hang any bands like ours which it could find, and said we had no time to lose. Farmer Mason was in a flurry this time, himself. He hurried us out of the house with all haste, and sent one of his negroes with us to show us where to hide ourselves and our telltale guns among the ravines half a mile away. It was raining heavily.

We struck down the lane, then across some rocky pasture-land which offered good advantages for stumbling; consequently we were down in the mud most of the time, and every time a man went down he blackguarded the war, and the people that started it, and everybody connected with it, and gave himself the master dose of all for being so foolish as to go into it. At last we reached the wooded mouth of a ravine, and there we huddled ourselves under the streaming trees, and sent the negro back home. It was a dismal and heart-breaking time. We were like to be drowned with the rain, deafened with the howling wind and the booming thunder, and blinded by the lightning. It was indeed a wild night. The drenching we were getting was misery enough, but a deeper misery still was the reflection that the halter might end us before we were a day older. A death of this shameful sort had not occurred to us as being among the possibilities of war. It took the romance all out of the campaign, and turned our dreams of glory into a repulsive nightmare. As for doubting that so barbarous an order had been given, not one of us did that.

The long night wore itself out at last, and then the negro came to us with the news that the alarm had manifestly been a false one, and that breakfast would soon be ready. Straightway we were light-hearted again, and the world was bright, and life as full of hope and promise as ever—for we were young then. How long ago that was! Twenty-four years.

The mongrel child of philology named the night's refuge Camp Devastation, and no soul objected. The Masons gave us a Missouri country breakfast, in Missourian abundance, and we needed it: hot biscuits; hot "wheat bread" prettily criss-crossed in a lattice pattern on top; hot corn pone; fried chicken; bacon, coffee, eggs, milk, buttermilk, etc.;—and the world may be confidently challenged to furnish the equal to such a breakfast, as it is cooked in the South.

We staid several days at Mason's; and after all these years the memory of the dullness, the stillness and lifelessness of that slumberous farm-house still oppresses my spirit as with a sense of the presence of death and mourning. There was nothing to do, nothing to think about; there was no interest in life. The male part of the household were away in the fields all day, the women were busy and out of our sight; there was no sound but the plaintive wailing of a spinning-wheel, forever moaning out from some distant room,—the most lonesome sound in nature, a sound steeped and sodden with homesickness and the emptiness of life. The family went to bed about dark every night, and as we were not invited to intrude any new customs, we naturally followed theirs. Those nights were a hundred years long to youths accustomed to being up till twelve. We lay awake and miserable till that hour every time, and grew old and decrepit waiting through the still eternities for the clock-strikes. This was no place for town boys. So at last it was with something very like joy that we received news that the enemy were on our track again. With a new birth of the old warrior spirit, we sprang to our places in line of battle and fell back on Camp Ralls.

Captain Lyman had taken a hint from Mason's talk, and he now gave orders that our camp should be guarded against surprise by the posting of pickets. I was ordered to place a picket at the forks of the road in Hyde's prairie. Night shut down black and threatening. I told Sergeant Bowers to go out to that place and stay till midnight; and, just as I was expecting, he said he wouldn't do it. I tried to get others to go, but all refused. Some excused themselves on account of the weather; but the rest were frank enough to say they wouldn't go in any kind of weather. This kind of thing sounds odd now, and impossible, but there was no surprise in it at the time. On the contrary, it seemed a perfectly natural thing to do. There were scores of little camps scattered over Missouri where the same thing was happening. These camps were composed of young men who had been born and reared to a sturdy independence, and who did not know what it meant to be ordered around by Tom, Dick, and Harry, whom they had known familiarly all their lives, in the village or on the farm. It is quite within the probabilities that this same thing was happening all over the South. James Redpath recognized the justice of this assumption, and furnished the following instance in support of it. During a short stay in East Tennessee he was in a citizen colonel's tent one day, talking, when a big private appeared at the door, and without salute or other circumlocution said to the colonel:

"Say, Jim, I'm a-goin' home for a few days."

"What for?"

"Well, I hain't be'en there for a right smart while, and I'd like to see how things is comin' on."

"How long are you going to be gone?"

" 'Bout two weeks."

"Well, don't be gone longer than that; and get back sooner if you can."

That was all, and the citizen officer resumed his conversation where the private had broken it off. This was in the first months of the war, of course. The camps in our part of Missouri were under Brigadier-General Thomas H. Harris. He was a townsman of ours, a first-rate fellow, and well liked; but we had all familiarly known him as the sole and modest-salaried operator in our telegraph office, where he had to send about one dispatch a week in ordinary times, and two when there was a rush of business; consequently, when he appeared in our midst one day, on the wing, and delivered a military command of some sort, in a large military fashion, nobody was surprised at the response which he got from the assembled soldiery:

"Oh, now, what'll you take to *don't*, Tom Harris!"

It was quite the natural thing. One might justly imagine that we were hopeless material for war. And so we seemed, in our ignorant state; but there were those among us who afterward learned the grim trade; learned to obey like machines; became valuable soldiers; fought all through the war, and came out at the end with excellent records. One of the very boys who refused to go out on picket duty that night, and called me an ass for thinking he would expose himself to danger in such a foolhardy way, had become distinguished for intrepidity before he was a year older.

I did secure my picket that night—not by authority, but by diplomacy. I got Bowers to go, by agreeing to exchange ranks with him for the time being, and go along and stand the watch with him as his subordinate. We staid out there a couple of dreary hours in the pitchy darkness and the rain, with nothing to modify the dreariness but Bowers's monotonous growlings at the war and the weather; then we began to nod, and presently found it next to impossible to stay in the saddle; so we gave up the tedious job, and went back to the camp without waiting for the relief guard. We rode into camp without interruption or objection from anybody, and the enemy could have done the same, for there were no sentries. Everybody was asleep; at midnight there was nobody to send out another picket, so none was sent. We never tried to establish a watch at night again, as far as I remember, but we generally kept a picket out in the daytime.

In that camp the whole command slept on the corn in the big corn-crib; and there was usually a general row before morning, for the place was full of rats, and they would scramble over the boys' bodies and faces, annoying and irritating everybody; and now and then they would bite some one's toe, and the person who owned the toe would start up and magnify his English and begin to throw corn in the dark. The ears were half as heavy as bricks, and when they struck they hurt. The persons struck would respond, and inside of five minutes every man would be locked in a death-grip with his neighbor. There was a grievous deal of blood shed in the corn-crib, but this was all that was spilt while I was in the war. No, that is not quite true. But for one circumstance it would have been all. I will come to that now.

Our scares were frequent. Every few days rumors

would come that the enemy were approaching. In these cases we always fell back on some other camp of ours; we never staid where we were. But the rumors always turned out to be false; so at last even we began to grow indifferent to them. One night a negro was sent to our corn-crib with the same old warning: the enemy was hovering in our neighborhood. We all said let him hover. We resolved to stay still and be comfortable. It was a fine warlike resolution, and no doubt we all felt the stir of it in our veins—for a moment. We had been having a very jolly time, that was full of horse-play and school-boy hilarity; but that cooled down now, and presently the fast-waning fire of forced jokes and forced laughs died out altogether, and the company became silent. Silent and nervous. And soon uneasy—worried—apprehensive. We had said we would stay, and we were committed. We could have been persuaded to go, but there was nobody brave enough to suggest it. An almost noiseless movement presently began in the dark, by a general but unvoiced impulse. When the movement was completed, each man knew that he was not the only person who had crept to the front wall and had his eye at a crack between the logs. No, we were all there; all there with our hearts in our throats, and staring out toward the sugar-troughs where the forest foot-path came through. It was late, and there was a deep woodsy stillness everywhere. There was a veiled moonlight, which was only just strong enough to enable us to mark the general shape of objects. Presently a muffled sound caught our ears, and we recognized it as the hoof-beats of a horse or horses. And right away a figure appeared in the forest path;

it could have been made of smoke, its mass had so little sharpness of outline. It was a man on horseback; and it seemed to me that there were others behind him. I got hold of a gun in the dark, and pushed it through a crack between the logs, hardly knowing what I was doing, I was so dazed with fright. Somebody said "Fire!" I pulled the trigger. I seemed to see a hundred flashes and hear a hundred reports, then I saw the man fall down out of the saddle. My first feeling was of surprised gratification; my first impulse was an apprentice-sportsman's impulse to run and pick up his game. Somebody said, hardly audibly, "Good—we've got him!—wait for the rest." But the rest did not come. We waited—listened—still no more came. There was not a sound, not the whisper of a leaf; just perfect stillness; an uncanny kind of stillness, which was all the more uncanny on account of the damp, earthy, late-night smells now rising and pervading it. Then, wondering, we crept stealthily out, and approached the man. When we got to him the moon revealed him distinctly. He was lying on his back, with his arms abroad; his mouth was open and his chest heaving with long gasps, and his white shirt-front was all splashed with blood. The thought shot through me that I was a murderer; that I had killed a man—a man who had never done me any harm. That was the coldest sensation that ever went through my marrow. I was down by him in a moment, helplessly stroking his forehead; and I would have given anything then—my own life freely—to make him again what he had been five minutes before. And all the boys seemed to be feeling in the same way; they hung over him, full of pitying interest, and tried all they could to help him, and said all sorts of regretful things. They had forgotten all about the enemy; they thought only of this one forlorn unit of the foe. Once my imagination persuaded me that the dying man gave me a reproachful look out of his shadowy eyes, and it seemed to me that I could rather he had stabbed me than done that. He muttered and mumbled like a dreamer in his sleep, about his wife and his child; and I thought with a new despair, "This thing that I have done does not end with him; it falls upon *them* too, and they never did me any harm, any more than he."

In a little while the man was dead. He was killed in war; killed in fair and legitimate war; killed in battle, as you may say; and yet he was as sincerely mourned by the opposing force as if he had been their brother. The boys stood there a half hour sorrowing over him, and recalling the details of the tragedy, and wondering who he might be, and if he were a spy, and saying that if it were to do over again they would not hunt him unless he attacked them first. It soon came out that mine was not the only shot fired; there were five others,—a division of the guilt which was a grateful relief to me, since it in some degree lightened and diminished the burden I was carrying. There were six shots fired at once; but I was not in my right mind at the time, and my heated imagination had magnified my one shot into a volley.

The man was not in uniform, and was not armed. He was a stranger in the country; that was all we ever found out about him. The thought of him got to preying upon me every night; I could not get rid of it. I could not drive it away, the taking of that unoffending life seemed such a wanton thing. And it seemed an epitome of war; that all war must be just that—the killing of strangers against whom you feel no personal animosity; strangers whom, in other circumstances, you would help if you found them in trouble, and who would help you if you needed it. My campaign was spoiled. It seemed to me that I was not rightly equipped for this awful business; that war was intended for men, and I for a child's nurse. I resolved to retire from this avocation of sham soldiership while I could save some remnant of my self-respect. These morbid thoughts clung to me against reason; for at bottom I did not believe I had touched that man. The law of probabilities decreed me guiltless of his blood; for in all my small experience with guns I had never hit anything I had tried to hit, and I knew I had done my best to hit him. Yet there was no solace in the thought. Against a diseased imagination, demonstration goes for nothing.

The rest of my war experience was of a piece with what I have already told of it. We kept monotonously falling back upon one camp or another, and eating up the country. I marvel now at the patience of the farmers and their families. They ought to have shot us; on the contrary, they were as hospitably kind and courteous to us as if we had deserved it. In one of these camps we found Ab Grimes, an Upper Mississippi pilot, who afterwards became famous as a dare-devil rebel spy, whose career bristled with desperate adventures. The look and style of his comrades suggested that they had not come into the war to play, and their deeds made good the conjecture later. They were fine horsemen and good revolver-shots; but their favorite arm was the lasso. Each had one at his pommel, and could snatch a man out of the saddle with it every time, on a full gallop, at any reasonable distance.

In another camp the chief was a fierce and profane old blacksmith of sixty, and he had furnished his twenty recruits with gigantic home-made bowie-knives, to be swung with the two hands, like the *machetes* of the Isthmus. It was a grisly spectacle to see that earnest band practicing their murderous cuts and slashes under the eye of that remorseless old fanatic.

The last camp which we fell back upon was in a hollow near the village of Florida, where I was born —in Monroe County. Here we were warned, one day, that a Union colonel was sweeping down on us with a whole regiment at his heels. This looked decidedly serious. Our boys went apart and consulted; then we went back and told the other companies present that the war was a disappointment to us and we were going to disband. They were getting ready, themselves, to fall back on some place or other, and were only waiting for General Tom Harris, who was expected to arrive at any moment; so they tried to persuade us to wait a little while, but the majority of us said no, we were accustomed to falling back, and didn't need any of Tom Harris's help; we could get along perfectly well without him—and save time too. So about half of our fifteen, including myself, mounted and left on the instant; the others yielded to persuasion and staid—staid through the war.

An hour later we met General Harris on the road, with two or three people in his company—his staff, probably, but we could not tell; none of them were in uniform; uniforms had not come into vogue among us yet. Harris ordered us back; but we told him there was a Union colonel coming with a whole regiment in his wake, and it looked as if there was going to be a disturbance; so we had concluded to go home. He raged a little, but it was of no use; our minds were made up. We had done our share; had killed one man, exterminated one army, such as it was; let him go and kill the rest, and that would end the war. I did not see that brisk young general again until last year; then he was wearing white hair and whiskers.

In time I came to know that Union colonel whose coming frightened me out of the war and crippled the Southern cause to that extent—General Grant. I came within a few hours of seeing him when he was as unknown as I was myself; at a time when anybody could have said, "Grant?—Ulysses S. Grant? I do not remember hearing the name before." It seems difficult to realize that there was once a time when such a remark could be rationally made; but there *was*, and I was within a few miles of the place and the occasion too, though proceeding in the other direction.

The thoughtful will not throw this war-paper of mine lightly aside as being valueless. It has this value: it is a not unfair picture of what went on in many and many a militia camp in the first months of the rebellion, when the green recruits were without discipline, without the steadying and heartening influence of trained leaders; when all their circumstances were new and strange, and charged with exaggerated terrors, and before the invaluable experience of actual collision in the field had turned them from rabbits into soldiers. If this side of the picture of that early day has not before been put into history, then history has been to that degree incomplete, for it had and has its rightful place there. There was more Bull Run material scattered through the early camps of this country than exhibited itself at Bull Run. And yet it learned its trade presently, and helped to fight the great battles later. I could have become a soldier myself, if I had waited. I had got part of it learned; I knew more about retreating than the man that invented retreating.

As Regards Patriotism
(1900?)

It is agreed, in this country, that if a man can arrange his religion so that it perfectly satisfies his conscience, it is not incumbent upon him to care whether the arrangement is satisfactory to any one else or not.

In Austria and some other countries this is not the case. There the State arranges a man's religion for him, he has no voice in it himself.

Patriotism is merely a religion—love of country, worship of country, devotion to the country's flag and honor and welfare.

In absolute monarchies it is furnished from the Throne, cut and dried, to the subject; in England and America it is furnished, cut and dried, to the citizen by the politician and the newspaper.

The newspaper-and-politician-manufactured Patriot often gags in private over his dose; but he takes it, and keeps it on his stomach the best he can. Blessed are the meek.

Sometimes, in the beginning of an insane and shabby political upheaval, he is strongly moved to revolt, but he doesn't do it—he knows better. He knows that his maker would find it out—the maker of his Patriotism, the windy and incoherent six-dollar sub-editor of his village newspaper—and would bray out in print and call him a Traitor. And how dreadful that would be. It makes him tuck his tail between his legs and shiver. We all know—the reader knows it quite well—that two or three years ago nine-tenths of the human tails in England and America performed just that act. Which is to say, nine-tenths of the Patriots in England and America turned Traitor to keep from being called Traitor. Isn't it true? You know it to be true. Isn't it curious?

Yet it was not a thing to be very seriously ashamed of. A man can seldom—very, very seldom—fight a winning fight against his training; the odds are too heavy. For many a year—perhaps always—the training of the two nations had been dead against independence in political thought, persistently inhospitable toward Patriotism manufactured on a man's own premises, Patriotism reasoned out in the man's own head and fire-assayed and tested and proved in his own conscience. The resulting Patriotism was a shop-worn product procured at second hand. The Patriot did not know just how or when or where he got his opinions, neither did he care, so long as he was with what seemed the majority—which was the main thing, the safe thing, the comfortable thing. Does the reader believe he knows three men who have actual reasons for their pattern of Patriotism—and can furnish them? Let him not examine, unless he wants to be disappointed. He will be likely to find that his men got their Patriotism at the public trough, and had no hand in their preparation themselves.

Training does wonderful things. It moved the people of this country to oppose the Mexican war; then moved them to fall in with what they supposed was the opinion of the majority—majority-Patriotism is the customary Patriotism—and go down there and fight. Before the Civil War it made the North indifferent to slavery and friendly to the slave interest; in that interest it made Massachusetts hostile to the American flag, and she would not allow it to be hoisted on her State House—in her eyes it was the flag of a faction. Then by and by, training swung Massachusetts the other way, and she went raging South to fight under that very flag and against that foretime protected-interest of hers.

Training made us nobly anxious to free Cuba; training made us give her a noble promise; training has enabled us to take it back. Long training made us revolt at the idea of wantonly taking any weak nation's country and liberties away from it, a short training has made us glad to do it, and proud of having done it. Training made us loathe Weyler's cruel concentration camps,* training has persuaded us to prefer them to any other device for winning the love of our "wards."

There is nothing that training cannot do. Nothing is above its reach or below it. It can turn bad morals to good, good morals to bad; it can destroy principles, it can re-create them; it can debase angels to men and lift men to angelship. And it can do any one of these miracles in a year—even in six months.

Then men can be trained to manufacture their own Patriotism. They can be trained to labor it out in

* Valeriano Weyler y Nicolau was the Spanish military governor of Cuba in 1896 and 1897 until he was recalled from the post in October as a result of American protest against his ruthless administration. (F.A.)

their own heads and hearts, and in the privacy and independence of their own premises. It can train them to stop taking it by command, as the Austrian takes his religion.

Passage from "Glances at History (Suppressed)" Date, 9th Century (1906?)

The original title for this piece, "First Fall of the Great Republic," was canceled by Mark Twain. The present title originally appeared as the subtitle. There is no record of Mark Twain's further plans for a book called "Glances at History" nor is there any explanation for his decision to pretend that it had been "suppressed" other than his fondness for the idea that his writings which dealt with religious and political subjects were too iconoclastic for publication. Very probably this fragment was, as Bernard DeVoto identified it, a part of the rambling "Papers of the Adam Family." Like "Extract from Article in 'The Radical,' Jan., 916," which appears later in this volume, the "Passage" begins abruptly. The person supposed to have made the original speech is not further identified, but the content of the speech vividly presents Mark Twain's view of "an unjust and trivial war," as he viewed American intervention in the Philippines at the turn of the century.

. . . In a speech which he made more than 500 years ago, and which has come down to us intact, he said:

We, free citizens of the Great Republic, feel an honest pride in her greatness, her strength, her just and gentle government, her wide liberties, her honored name, her stainless history, her unsmirched flag, her hands clean from oppression of the weak and from malicious conquest, her hospitable door that stands open to the hunted and the persecuted of all nations; we are proud of the judicious respect in which she is held by the monarchies which hem her in on every side, and proudest of all of that lofty patriotism which we inherited from our fathers, which we have kept pure, and which won our liberties in the beginning and has preserved them unto this day. While that patriotism endures the Republic is safe, her greatness is secure, and against them the powers of the earth cannot prevail.

I pray you to pause and consider. Against our traditions we are now entering upon an unjust and trivial war, a war against a helpless people, and for a base object—robbery. At first our citizens spoke out against this thing, by an impulse natural to their training. To-day they have turned, and their voice is the other way. What caused the change? Merely a politician's trick—a high-sounding phrase, a blood-stirring phrase which turned their uncritical heads: *Our Country, right or wrong!* An empty phrase, a silly phrase. It was shouted by every newspaper, it was thundered from the pulpit, the Superintendent of Public Instruction placarded it in every schoolhouse in the land, the War Department inscribed it upon the flag. And every man who failed to shout it or who was silent, was proclaimed a traitor—none but those others were patriots. To be a patriot, one had to say, and keep on saying, "Our Country, right or wrong," and urge on the little war. Have you not perceived that that phrase is an insult to the nation?

For in a Republic, who *is* "the country?" Is it the Government which is for the moment in the saddle? Why, the Government is merely a *servant*—merely a temporary servant; it cannot be its prerogative to determine what is right and what is wrong, and decide who is a patriot and who isn't. Its function is to obey orders, not originate them. Who, then, is "the country?" Is it the newspaper? is it the pulpit? is it the school-superintendent? Why, these are mere parts of the country, not the whole of it; they have not command, they have only their little share in the command. They are but one in the thousand; it is in the thousand that command is lodged; *they* must determine what is right and what is wrong; they must decide who is a patriot and who isn't.

Who are the thousand—that is to say, who are "the country?" In a monarchy, the King and his family are the country; in a republic it is the common voice of the people. Each of you, for himself, by himself and on his own responsibility, must speak. And it is a solemn and weighty responsibility, and not lightly to be flung aside at the bullying of pulpit, press, government, or the empty catchphrases of politicians. Each must for himself alone decide what is right and what is wrong, and which course is patriotic and which isn't. You cannot shirk this and be a man. To decide it against your convictions is to be an unqualified and inexcusable traitor, both to yourself and to your country, let men label you as they may. If you alone of all the nation shall decide one way, and that way be the right way according to your convictions of the right, you have done your duty by yourself and by your country—hold up your head! you have nothing to be ashamed of.

Only when a republic's *life* is in danger should a man uphold his government when it is in the wrong. There is no other time.

This republic's life is not in peril. The nation has sold its honor for a phrase. It has swung itself loose from its safe anchorage and is drifting, its helm is in pirate hands. The stupid phrase needed help, and it got another one: "Even if the war be wrong we are in it and must fight it out: *we cannot retire from it without dishonor.*" Why, not even a burglar could have said it better. We cannot withdraw from this sordid raid because to grant peace to those little people upon their terms—independence—would dishonor us. You have flung away Adam's phrase—you should take it up and examine it again. He said, "*An inglorious peace is better than a dishonorable war.*"

You have planted a seed, and it will grow.

From *Mark Twain's Mysterious Stranger Manuscripts:* "The Chronicle of Young Satan" (1900)

From 1897 through 1908 Mark Twain worked at three major manuscripts which were built around the visit of a "mysterious stranger"—called Satan in the extracts quoted—to a rural village. "The Chronicle of Young Satan," the first of the three attempts, is set in Austria in 1702. Mark Twain's ultimate purpose in these parables is to reveal the moral squalor and the physical misery in which man in his eyes had always existed. The immediate reason for writing the following extracts in 1900 was military ferment in China, South Africa, and the Philippines.

I. History of War

One day, a little while after this, Satan appeared again. We were always watching out for him—Seppi and I—and longing for him; for life was never very stagnant when he was by. He came upon us at that place in the woods where we had first met him. Being boys, we wanted to be entertained, and we asked him to do a show for us.

"Very well," he said, "would you like to see a history of the progress of the human race?—its development of that product which it calls Civilization?"

We said we should.

So, with a thought, he turned the place into the Garden of Eden, and we saw Abel praying by his altar; then Cain came walking toward him with his club, and did not seem to see us, and would have stepped on my foot if I had not drawn it in. He spoke to his brother in a language which we did not understand; then he grew violent and threatening, and we knew what was going to happen, and turned away our heads for the moment; but we heard the crash of the blows and heard the shrieks and the groans; then there was silence, and we saw Abel lying in his blood and gasping out his life, and Cain standing over him and looking down at him, vengeful and unrepentant.

Then the vision vanished, and was followed by a long series of unknown wars, murders and massacres. Next, we had the Flood, and the Ark tossing around in the stormy waters, with lofty mountains in the distance showing veiled and dim through the rain. Satan said—

"The progress of your race was not satisfactory. It it is to have another chance, now."

The scene changed, and we saw Noah lying drunk on Ararat.

Next, we had Sodom and Gomorrah, and "the attempt to discover two or three respectable persons there," as Satan described it. Next, Lot and his daughters in the cave.

Next came the Hebraic wars, and we saw the victors massacre the survivors and their cattle, and save the young girls alive and distribute them around.

Next, we had Jael; and saw her slip into the tent and drive the nail into the temples of her sleeping guest; and we were so close that when the blood gushed out it trickled in a little red stream to our feet and we could have stained our hands in it if we had wanted to.

Next we had Egyptian wars, Greek wars, Roman wars, hideous drenchings of the earth with blood; and we saw the treacheries of the Romans toward the Carthaginians, and the sickening spectacle of the massacre of those brave people. Also we saw Caesar invade Britain—"not that those barbarians had done him any harm, but because he wanted their land, and desired to confer the blessings of civilization upon their widows and orphans," as Satan explained.

Next Christianity was born. Then, ages of Europe passed in review before us, and we saw Christianity and Civilization march hand in hand through those ages, "leaving famine and death and desolation in their wake, and other signs of the progress of the human race," as Satan observed.

Then the Holy Inquisition was born; "another step in your progress," Satan said. He showed us thousands of torn and mutilated heretics shrieking under the torture, and other thousands and thousands of heretics and witches burning at the stake, "always in the pleasant shade flung by the peaceful banner of the cross," as Satan remarked. And in the midst of these fearful spectacles, as an incidental matter, we had a marvelous nightshow, by the light of flitting and flying torches—the butchery of Christian by Christian in France on Bartholomew's Day.

And always we had wars, and more wars, and still other wars—all over Europe, all over the world. "Sometimes in the private interest of royal families,"

Satan said, "sometimes to get more land, sometimes to crush a weak nation; but never a war started by the aggressor for any clean purpose—there is no such war in the history of your race."

"Now," said Satan, "you have seen your progress down to the present, and you must confess that it is wonderful—in its way. We must now exhibit the future. In a year or two we shall have Blenheim and Ramillies. Look!"

He showed us those awful slaughters.

"You perceive," he said, "that you have made continual progress. Cain did his murder with a club; the Hebrews did their murders with javelins and swords; the Greeks and Romans added protective armor and the fine arts of military organization and generalship; the Christian has added guns and gunpowder; two centuries from now he will have so greatly improved the deadly effectiveness of his weapons of slaughter that all men will confess that without the Christian Civilization war must have remained a poor and trifling thing to the end of time. In that day the lands and peoples of the whole pagan world will be at the mercy of the sceptred bandits of Europe, and they will take them. Furnishing in return, the blessings of civilization.

"Nine years from now a Prussian prince will be born who will steal Silesia; plunge several nations into bloody and desolating wars; lead a life of treachery and general and particular villainy, and be admiringly called 'the Great.' Sixty-six years from now a Corsican will be born who will deluge Europe with blood and spread the Christian civilization far and wide. He also will be called 'the Great.' A trifle before his day, England will begin to swallow India. In his early manhood there will be a Revolution in France whose bloody exhibitions will be a more terrible thing to see than even France will have known since the Bartholomew Day. All through the next century there will be wars—wars everywhere in the earth. Wars for gain—each one a crime on the part of the provoker of it. An English queen will reign more than sixty years, and fight more than sixty wars during her reign—spreading civilization generously; also with profit. England, desiring a weak State's diamond mines, will take them—by robbery, but courteously. Desiring another weak State's gold mines, her statesmen will try to seize them by piracy; failing, they will manufacture a war and take them in that way; and with them the small State's independence.

"The Christian missionary will exasperate the Chinese; they will kill him in a riot. They will have to pay for him, in territory, cash, and churches, sixty-two million times his value. This will exasperate the Chinese still more, and they will injudiciously rise in revolt against the insults and oppressions of the intruder. This will be Europe's chance to interfere and swallow China, and her band of royal Christian pirates will not waste it. Now then, I will show you this long array of crimson spectacles, so that you can note the progress of civilization from the time that Cain began it down to a period a couple of centuries hence."

Then he began to laugh in the most unfeeling way, and make fun of the human race, although he knew that what he had been saying shamed us and wounded us. No one but an angel could have acted so; but suffering is nothing to them, they do not know what it is, except by hearsay.

More than once Seppi and I had tried in a humble and diffident way to convert him; and as he had remained silent we had taken his silence as a sort of encouragement; necessarily, then, this talk of his was a disappointment to us, for it showed that we had made no deep impression upon him. The thought made us sad, and we knew, then, how the missionary must feel when he has been cherishing a glad hope and has seen it blighted. We kept our grief to ourselves, knowing that this was not the time to continue our work.

Satan laughed his unkind laugh to a finish, then he said—

"It is a remarkable progress. In five or six thousand years five or six high civilizations have risen, flourished, commanded the wonder of the world, then faded out and disappeared; and not one of them except the latest, ever invented any sweeping and adequate way to kill people. They all did their best, to kill being the chiefest ambition of the human race and the earliest incident in its history, but only the Christian Civilization has scored a triumph to be proud of. Two centuries from now it will be recognized that all the competent killers are Christian; then the pagan world will go to school to the Christian: not to acquire his religion, but his guns. The Turk and the Chinaman will buy those, to kill missionaries and converts with."

By this time his theater was at work again: and before our eyes nation after nation drifted by, during two centuries, a mighty procession, an endless procession, raging, struggling, wallowing through seas of blood, smothered in battle-smoke through which the flags glinted and the red jets from the cannon darted; and always we heard the thunder of the guns and the cries of the dying.

"And what does it amount to?" said Satan, with his evil chuckle. "Nothing at all. You gain nothing; you always come out where you went in. For a million years the race has gone on monotonously propagating itself and monotonously re-performing this dull nonsense—to what end? No wisdom can guess! Who gets a profit out of it? Nobody but a parcel of usurping little monarchs and nobilities who despise you; would feel defiled if you touched them; would shut the door in your face if you proposed to call; whom you slave for, fight for, die for, and are not ashamed of it, but proud; whose existence is a perpetual insult to you and you are afraid to resent it; who are mendicants supported by your alms, yet assume toward you the airs of benefactor toward beggar; who address you in the language of master to slave and are answered in the language of slave to master; who are worshiped by you with your mouth, while in your hearts—if you have one—you despise yourselves for it. The first man was a hypocrite and a coward, qualities which have not yet failed in his line: it is the foundation upon which all civilizations have been built. Drink to their perpetuation! drink to their augmentation! drink to—"

Then he saw by our faces how much we were hurt, and he cut his sentence short and stopped chuckling, and his manner changed. He said gently—

"No, we will drink each other's health, and let civilization go." . . .

II. Dishonorable War

"Oh, it's true. I know your race. It is made up of sheep. It is governed by minorities, seldom or never by majorities. It suppresses its feelings and its beliefs and follows the handful that makes the most noise. Sometimes the noisy handful is right, sometimes wrong; but no matter, the crowd follows it. The vast majority of the race, whether savage or civilized, are secretly kind-hearted, and shrink from inflicting pain; but in the presence of the aggressive and pitiless minority they don't dare to assert themselves. Think of it! one kind-hearted creature spies upon another, and sees to it that he loyally helps in iniquities which revolt both of them. Speaking as an expert, I *know* that ninety-nine out of a hundred of your race were strongly against the killing of witches when that foolishness was first agitated by a handful of pious lunatics in the long ago. And I know that even to-day, after ages of transmitted prejudice and silly teaching, only one person in twenty puts any real heart into the harrying of a witch. And yet apparently *everybody* hates witches and wants them killed. Some day a handful will rise up on the other side and make the most noise—perhaps even a single daring man with a big voice and a determined front will do it—and in a week all the sheep will wheel and follow him, and witch-hunting will come to a sudden end. In fact this happened within these ten years, in a little country called New England.

"Monarchies, aristocracies and religions are all based upon that large defect in your race—the individual's distrust of his neighbor, and his desire, for safety's or comfort's sake, to stand well in his neighbor's eyes. These institutions will always remain, always flourish, and always oppress you, affront you and degrade you, because you will always be and remain slaves of minorities. There was never a country where the majority of the people were in their secret hearts loyal to either of these institutions."

I did not like to hear our race called sheep, and said I did not think they were.

"Still, it is true, lamb," said Satan. "Look at you in war—what mutton you are, and how ridiculous."

"In war? How?"

"There has never been a just one, never an honorable one—on the part of the instigator of the war. I can see a million years ahead, and this rule will never change in so many as half a dozen instances. The loud little handful—as usual—will shout for the war. The pulpit will—warily and cautiously—object—at first; the great big dull bulk of the nation will rub its sleepy eyes and try to make out why there should be a war, and will say, earnestly and indignantly, "It is unjust and dishonorable, and there is no necessity for it." Then the handful will shout louder. A few fair men on the other side will argue and reason against the war with speech and pen, and at first will have a hearing and be applauded; but it will not last long; those others will out-shout them, and presently the anti-war audiences will thin out and lose popularity. Before long you will see this curious thing: the speakers stoned from the platform and free speech strangled, by hordes of furious men who in their secret hearts are still at one with those stoned speakers,—as earlier,—but do not dare to say so! And now the whole nation—pulpit and all—will take up the war-cry, and shout itself hoarse, and mob any honest man who ventures to open his mouth; and presently such mouths will cease to open. Next, the statesmen will invent cheap lies, putting the blame upon the nation that is attacked, and every man will be glad of those conscience-soothing falsities, and will diligently study them, and refuse to examine any refutations of them; and thus he will by and by convince himself that the war *is* just, and will thank God for the better sleep he enjoys after this process of grotesque self-deception."

Letter to Sylvester Baxter
(1889)

Sylvester Baxter was preparing to write a review of Mark Twain's "forthcoming book," A Connecticut Yankee in King Arthur's Court. *The two men were currently corresponding enthusiastically about evidence of political change in both national and international affairs. Mark Twain's letter of 20 November 1889 was inspired by the news that Emperor Dom Pedro II of Brazil had been overthrown on 15 November.*

DEAR MR. BAXTER:

Another throne has gone down, and I swim in oceans of satisfaction. I wish I might live fifty-years longer; I believe I should see the thrones of Europe selling at auction for old iron. I believe I should really see the end of what is surely the grotesquest of all the swindles ever invented by man—monarchy. It is enough to make a graven image laugh, to see apparently rational people, away down here in this wholesome and merciless slaughter-day for shams, still mouthing empty reverence for those moss-backed frauds and scoundrelisms, hereditary kingship and so-called "nobility." It is enough to make the monarchs and nobles themselves laugh—and in private they do; there can be no question about that. I think there is only one funnier thing, and that is the spectacle of these bastard Americans—these Hamersleys and Huntingtons and such—offering cash, encumbered by themselves, for rotten carcases and stolen titles. When our great brethren the dis-enslaved Brazilians frame their Declaration of Independence, I hope they will insert this missing link: "We hold these truths to be self-evident: that all monarchs are usurpers, and descendants of usurpers; for the reason that no throne was ever set up in this world by the will, freely exercised, of the only body possessing the legitimate right to set it up—the numerical mass of the nation."

You already have the advance sheets of my forthcoming book in your hands. If you will turn to about the five hundredth page, you will find a state paper of my Connecticut Yankee in which he announces the dissolution of King Arthur's monarchy and proclaims the English Republic. Compare it with the state paper which announces the downfall of the Brazilian monarchy and proclaims the Republic of the United States of Brazil, and stand by to defend the Yankee from plagiarism. There is merely a resemblance of ideas, nothing more. The Yankee's proclamation was already in print a week ago. This is merely one of those odd coincidences which are always turning up. Come, protect the Yank from that cheapest and easiest of all charges—plagiarism. Otherwise, you see, he will have to protect himself by charging approximate and indefinite plagiarism upon the official servants of our majestic twin down yonder, and then there might be war, or some similar annoyance.

Have you noticed the rumor that the Portuguese throne is unsteady and that the Portuguese slaves are getting restive? Also the rumor that the head slave-driver of Europe, Alexander III, has so reduced his usual monthly order for chains that the Russian foundries are running on only half time, now? Also that other rumor that English nobility acquired an added stench the other day—and had to ship it to India and the Continent because there wasn't any more room for it at home? * Things are working. By and by there is going to be an emigration, maybe. Of course we shall make no preparation; we never do. In a few years from now we shall have nothing but played-out kings and dukes on the police, and driving the horse-cars, and whitewashing fences, and in fact overcrowding all the avenues of unskilled labor; and then we shall wish, when it is too late,

* On November 10, 1889, the New York *Times* printed a column, "November London Gossip," which referred to an "extremely painful and revolting scandal which is being unearthed here by the authorities, and which involves a large number of men in the highest circles of English society." Lord Arthur Somerset "was allowed to get away" and "current rumor says that Prince Albert Victor [eldest son of Edward VII, at this time Prince of Wales] will not return from India until the matter is completely over and forgotten." The London *Times* printed guarded accounts of the charges and investigation throughout the first half of 1890 which indicate the scandal concerned a male bordello in Cleveland Street whose occupants were boys recruited from the London Post Office and whose patrons included several members of the English aristocracy. (F.A.)

that we had taken common and reasonable precautions, and drowned them at Castle Garden.

Truly yours,
MARK

P.S. I don't remember the terms of the Yankee's proclamation, but I have an impression that there is a sort of resemblance of ideas. Can't you put the two proclamations in the fatal "double columns" and charge the Brazilians with plagiarising the Yankee? —that is, if there is room to pretend a resemblance? Consider, the Yank was more than thirteen hundred years ahead of those Brazilian statesmen.

Letter to the Editor of *Free Russia* (1890)

Mark Twain's unmailed letter was apparently written in response to a request for a contribution accompanied by a copy of the journal. The quoted paragraph is clipped from the first page of the first issue, dated August 1890. Free Russia *was published in New York and London by the "Society of Friends of Russian Freedom." The July 1891 and subsequent issues include "Samuel L. Clemens" in a list of "American men and women whose sympathies are not restricted by geographical bounderies [sic] and whose hearts can beat for the suffering of others."*

TO THE EDITOR OF FREE RUSSIA:

I thank you for the compliment of your invitation to say something, but when I ponder the bottom paragraph on your first page, and then study your statement, on your third page, of the objects of the several Russian liberation-parties, I do not quite know how to proceed. Let me quote here the paragraph referred to:

But men's hearts are so made that the sight of one voluntary victim for a noble idea stirs them more deeply than the sight of a crowd submitting to a dire fate they cannot escape. Besides, foreigners could not see so clearly as the Russians how much the Government was responsible for the grinding poverty of the masses; nor could they very well realise the moral wretchedness imposed by that Government upon the whole of educated Russia. But the atrocities committed upon the defenceless prisoners are there in all their baseness, concrete and palpable, admitting of no excuse, no doubt or hesitation, crying out to the heart of humanity against Russian tyranny. And the Tzar's Government, stupidly confident in its apparently unassailable position, instead of taking warning from the first rebukes, seemed to mock this humanitarian age by the aggravation of brutalities. Not satisfied with slowly killing its prisoners, and with burying the flower of our young generation in the Siberian deserts, the Government of Alexander III resolved to break their spirit by deliberately submitting them to a regime of unheard-of brutality and degradation.

When one reads that paragraph in the glare of George Kennan's revelations, and considers how much it means; considers that all earthly figures fail to typify the Czar's government, and that one must descend into hell to find its counterpart, one turns hopefully to your statement of the objects of the several liberation-parties—and is disappointed. Apparently none of them can bear to think of losing the present hell entirely, they merely want the temperature cooled down a little.

I now perceive why all men are the deadly and uncompromising enemies of the rattlesnake: it is merely because the rattlesnake has not speech. Monarchy has speech, and by it has been able to persuade men that it differs somehow from the rattlesnake, has something valuable about it somewhere, something worth preserving, something even good and high and fine, when properly "modified," something entitling it to protection from the club of the first comer who catches it out of its hole. It seems a most strange delusion and not reconcilable with our superstition that man is a reasoning being. If a house is afire, we reason confidently that it is the first comer's plain duty to put the fire out in any way he can—drown it with water, blow it up with dynamite, use any and all means to stop the spread of the fire and save the rest of the city. What is the Czar of Russia but a house afire in the midst of a city of eighty millions of inhabitants? Yet instead of extinguishing him, together with his nest and system, the liberation-parties are all anxious to merely cool him down a little and keep him.

It seems to me that this is illogical—idiotic, in fact. Suppose you had this granite-hearted, bloody-jawed maniac of Russia loose in your house, chasing the helpless women and little children—your own. What would you do with him, supposing you had a shotgun? Well, he *is* loose in your house—Russia. And with your shotgun in your hand, you stand trying to think up ways to "modify" him.

Do those liberation-parties think that they can succeed in a project which has been attempted a million times in the history of the world and has never in one single instance been successful—the "modification" of a despotism by other means than bloodshed? They seem to think they can. My privilege to write these sanguinary sentences in soft security was bought for me by rivers of blood poured upon many fields, in many lands, but I possess not one single little paltry right or privilege that came to me as a result of petition, persuasion, agitation for reform, or any kindred method of procedure. When we consider that not even the most reasonable English monarchs ever yielded back a stolen public right until it was wrenched from them by bloody violence, is it rational to suppose that gentler methods can win privileges in Russia?

Of course I know that the properest way to demolish the Russian throne would be by revolution. But it is not possible to get up a revolution there; so the only thing left to do, apparently, is to keep the throne vacant by dynamite until a day when candidates shall decline with thanks. Then organize the Republic. And on the whole this method has some large advantages; for whereas a revolution destroys some lives which cannot well be spared, the dynamite way doesn't. Consider this: the conspirators against the Czar's life are caught in *every* rank of life, from the low to the high. And consider: if so many take an active part, where the peril is so dire, is this not evidence that the sympathizers who keep still and do not show their hands, are countless for multitude? Can you break the hearts of thousands of families with the awful Siberian exodus every year for generations and not eventually cover all Russia from limit to limit with bereaved fathers and mothers and brothers and sisters who secretly hate the perpetrator of this prodigious crime and hunger and thirst for his life? Do not you believe that if your wife or your child or your father was exiled to the mines of Siberia for some trivial utterance wrung from a smarting spirit by the Czar's intolerable tyranny, and you got a chance to kill him and did not do it, that you would always be ashamed to be in your own society the rest of your life? Suppose that that refined and lovely Russian lady who was lately stripped bare before a brutal soldiery and whipped to death by the Czar's hand in the person of the Czar's creature had been your wife, or your daughter or your sister, and to-day the Czar should pass within reach of your hand, how would you feel—and what would you do? Consider, that all over vast Russia, from boundary to boundary, a myriad of eyes filled with tears when that piteous news came, and through those tears that myriad of eyes saw, not that poor lady, but lost darlings of their own whose fate her fate brought back with new access of grief out of a black and bitter past never to be forgotten or forgiven.

If I am a Swinburnian—and clear to the marrow I am—I hold human nature in sufficient honor to believe there are eighty million mute Russians that are of the same stripe, and only one Russian family that isn't.

MARK TWAIN

Letter to William T. Stead
(1890)

Albert Bigelow Paine comments in his edition of Mark Twain's Letters, *where this was first printed, that "a project for world disarmament promulgated by the Czar of Russia would naturally interest Mark Twain, and when William T. Stead, of* The Review of Reviews, *cabled him for an opinion on the matter, he sent at first a brief word and on the same day followed it with more extended comment."*

Vienna, Jan. 9

DEAR MR. STEAD,—The Czar is ready to disarm: *I* am ready to disarm. Collect the *others,* it should not be much of a task now.

MARK TWAIN

No. 2.

DEAR MR. STEAD,—Peace by compulsion. That seems a better idea than the other. Peace by persuasion has a pleasant sound, but I think we should not be able to work it. We should have to tame the human race first, and history seems to show that that cannot be done. Can't we reduce the armaments little by little—on a pro rata basis—by concert of the powers? Can't we get four great powers to agree to reduce their strength 10 per cent a year and thrash the others into doing likewise? For, of course, we cannot expect all of the powers to be in their right minds at one time. It has been tried. We are not going to try to get all of them to go into the scheme peaceably, are we? In that case I must withdraw my influence; because, for business reasons, I must preserve the outward signs of sanity. Four is enough if they can be securely harnessed together. They can compel peace, and peace without compulsion would be against nature and not operative. A sliding scale of reduction of 10 per cent a year has a sort of plausible look, and I am willing to try that if three other powers will join. I feel sure that the armaments are now many times greater than necessary for the requirements of either peace or war. Take war-time for instance. Suppose circumstances made it necessary for us to fight another Waterloo, and that it would do what it did before—settle a large question and bring peace. I will guess that 400,000 men were on hand at Waterloo (I have forgotten the figures). In five hours they disabled 50,000 men. It took them that tedious, long time because the firearms delivered only two or three shots a minute. But we would do the work now as it was done at Omdurman, with shower guns, raining 600 balls a minute. Four men to a gun—is that the number? A hundred and fifty shots a minute per man. Thus a modern soldier is 149 Waterloo soldiers in one. Thus, also, we can now retain one man out of each 150 in service, disband the others, and fight our Waterloos just as effectively as we did eighty-five years ago. We should do the same beneficent job with 2,800 men now that we did with 400,000 then. The allies could take 1,400 of the men, and give Napoleon 1,400 and then whip him.

But instead what do we see? In war-time in Germany, Russia and France, taken together we find about 8 million men equipped for the field. Each man represents 149 Waterloo men, in usefulness and killing capacity. Altogether they constitute about 350 million Waterloo men, and there are not quite that many grown males of the human race now on this planet. Thus we have this insane fact—that whereas those three countries could arm 18,000 men with modern weapons and make them the equals of 3 million men of Napoleon's day, and accomplish with them all necessary war work, they waste their money and their prosperity creating forces of their populations in piling together 349,982,000 extra Waterloo equivalents which they would have no sort of use for if they would only stop drinking and sit down and cipher a little.

Perpetual peace we cannot have on any terms, I suppose; but I hope we can gradually reduce the war strength of Europe till we get it down to where it ought to be—20,000 men, properly armed. Then we can have all the peace that is worth while, and when we want a war anybody can afford it.

Vienna, January 9

P.S.—In the article I sent the figures are wrong—"350 million" ought to be 450 million; "349,982,000" ought to be 449,982,000, and the remark about the sum being a little more than the present number of males on the planet—that is wrong, of course; it represents really one and a half the existing males.

To the Person Sitting in Darkness
(1901)

Christmas will dawn in the United States over a people full of hope and aspiration and good cheer. Such a condition means contentment and happiness. The carping grumbler who may here and there go forth will find few to listen to him. The majority will wonder what is the matter with him and pass on. —New York Tribune, *on Christmas Eve.*

From *The Sun,* of New York:

The purpose of this article is not to describe the terrible offences against humanity committed in the name of Politics in some of the most notorious East Side districts. *They could not be described, even verbally.* But it is the intention to let the great mass of more or less careless citizens of this beautiful metropolis of the New World get some conception of the havoc and ruin wrought to man, woman and child in the most densely populated and least known section of the city. Name, date and place can be supplied to those of little faith—or to any man who feels himself aggrieved. It is a plain statement of record and observation, written without license and without garnish.

Imagine, if you can, a section of the city territory completely dominated by one man, without whose permission neither legitimate nor illegitimate business can be conducted; *where illegitimate business is encouraged and legitimate business discouraged;* where the respectable residents have to fasten their doors and windows summer nights and sit in their rooms with asphyxiating air and 100-degree temperature, rather than try to catch the faint whiff of breeze in their natural breathing places, the stoops of their homes; *where naked women dance by night in the streets, and unsexed men prowl like vultures through the darkness on "business"* not only permitted but encouraged by the police; *where the education of infants begins with the knowledge of prostitution* and the training of little girls is training in the arts of Phryne; where *American* girls brought up with the refinements of *American* homes are imported from small towns up-State, Massachusetts, Connecticut and New Jersey, and kept as virtually prisoners as if they were locked up behind jail bars until they have lost all semblance of womanhood; *where small boys are taught to solicit for the women of disorderly houses;* where there is an organized society of young men *whose sole business in life is to corrupt young girls and turn them over to bawdy houses;* where men walking with their wives along the street are openly insulted; *where children that have adult diseases are the chief patrons of the hospitals and dispensaries;* where it is the rule, rather than the exception, that *murder, rape, robbery and theft go unpunished*—in short where the Premium of the most awful forms of Vice is the Profit of the politicians.

The following news from China appeared in *The Sun,* of New York, on Christmas Eve. The italics are mine:

The Rev. Mr. Ament, of the American Board of Foreign Missions, has returned from a trip which he made for the purpose of collecting indemnities for damages done by Boxers. *Everywhere he went he compelled the*

Chinese to pay. He says that all his native Christians are now provided for. He had 700 of them under his charge, and 300 were killed. He has *collected 300 taels for each* of these murders, and has *compelled full payment for all the property belonging to Christians* that was destroyed. He also assessed *fines* amounting to THIRTEEN TIMES the amount of the indemnity. *This money will be used for the propagation of the Gospel.*

Mr. Ament declares that the compensation he has collected is *moderate,* when compared with the amount secured by the Catholics, who demand, in addition to money, *head for head.* They collect 500 taels for each murder of a Catholic. In the Wenchiu country, 680 Catholics were killed, and for this the European Catholics here demand 750,000 strings of cash and 680 *heads.*

In the course of a conversation, Mr. Ament referred to the attitude of the missionaries toward the Chinese. He said:

"I deny emphatically that the missionaries are *vindictive,* that they *generally* looted, or that they have done anything *since* the siege that the *circumstances did not demand.* I criticise the Americans. *The soft hand of the Americans is not as good as the mailed fist of the Germans.* If you deal with the Chinese with a soft hand they will take advantage of it."

The statement that the French Government will return the loot taken by the French soldiers, is the source of the greatest amusement here. The French soldiers were more systematic looters than the Germans, and it is a fact that to-day *Catholic Christians,* carrying French flags and armed with modern guns, *are looting villages* in the Province of Chili.

By happy luck, we get all these glad tidings on Christmas Eve—just in time to enable us to celebrate the day with proper gaiety and enthusiasm.

Our spirits soar, and we find we can even make jokes: Taels I win, Heads you lose.

Our Reverend Ament is the right man in the right place. What we want of our missionaries out there is, not that they shall merely represent in their acts and persons the grace and gentleness and charity and loving kindness of our religion, but that they shall also represent the American spirit. The oldest Americans are the Pawnees. Macaluml's History says:

When a white Boxer kills a Pawnee and destroys his property, the other Pawnees do not trouble to seek *him* out, they kill any white person that comes along; also, they make some white village pay deceased's heirs the full cash value of deceased, together with full cash value of the property destroyed; they also make the village pay, in addition, *thirteen times* the value of that property into a fund for the dissemination of the Pawnee religion, which they regard as the best of all religions for the softening and humanizing of the heart of man. It is their idea that it is only fair and right that the innocent should be made to suffer for the guilty, and that it is better that ninety and nine innocent should suffer than that one guilty person should escape.

Our Reverend Ament is justifiably jealous of those enterprising Catholics, who not only get big money for each lost convert, but get "head for head" besides. But he should soothe himself with the reflection that the entirety of their exactions are for their own pockets, whereas he, less selfishly, devotes only 300 taels per head to that service, and gives the whole vast thirteen repetitions of the property-indemnity to the service of propagating the Gospel.

His magnanimity has won him the approval of his nation, and will get him a monument. Let him be content with these rewards. We all hold him dear for manfully defending his fellow missionaries from exaggerated charges which were beginning to distress us, but which his testimony has so considerably modified that we can now contemplate them without noticeable pain. For now we know that, even before the siege, the missionaries were not "generally" out looting, and that, "since the siege," they have acted quite handsomely, except when "circumstances" crowded them. I am arranging for the monument. Subscriptions for it can be sent to the American Board; designs for it can be sent to me. Designs must allegorically set forth the Thirteen Reduplications of the Indemnity, and the Object for which they were exacted; as Ornaments, the designs must exhibit 680 Heads, so disposed as to give a pleasing and pretty effect; for the Catholics have done nicely, and are entitled to notice in the monument. Mottoes may be suggested, if any shall be discovered that will satisfactorily cover the ground.

Mr. Ament's financial feat of squeezing a thirteen-fold indemnity out of the pauper peasants to square other people's offenses, thus condemning them and their women and innocent little children to inevitable starvation and lingering death, in order that the blood-money so acquired might be *"used for the propagation of the Gospel,"* does not flutter my serenity; although the act and the words, taken together, concrete a blasphemy so hideous and so colossal that, without doubt, its mate is not findable in the history of this or of any other age. Yet, if a layman had done that thing and justified it with those words, I should have shuddered, I know. Or, if I had done the thing and said the words myself—however, the thought is unthinkable, irreverent as some imperfectly informed people think me. Sometimes an ordained minister sets out to be blasphemous. When this happens, the layman is out of the running; he stands no chance.

We have Mr. Ament's impassioned assurance that the missionaries are not "vindictive." Let us hope and pray that they will never become so, but will remain in the almost morbidly fair and just and gentle temper which is affording so much satisfaction to their brother and champion to-day.

The following is from the *New York Tribune* of Christmas Eve. It comes from that journal's Tokio correspondent. It has a strange and impudent sound, but the Japanese are but partially civilized as yet. When they become wholly civilized they will not talk so:

> The missionary question, of course, occupies a foremost place in the discussion. It is now felt as essential that the Western Powers take cognizance of the sentiment here, that religious invasions of Oriental countries by powerful Western organizations are tantamount to filibustering expeditions, and should not only be discountenanced, but that stern measures should be adopted for their suppression. The feeling here is that the missionary organizations constitute a constant menace to peaceful international relations.

Shall we? That is, shall we go on conferring our Civilization upon the peoples that sit in darkness, or shall we give those poor things a rest? Shall we bang right ahead in our old-time, loud, pious way, and commit the new century to the game; or shall we sober up and sit down and think it over first? Would it not be prudent to get our Civilization-tools together, and see how much stock is left on hand in the way of Glass Beads and Theology, and Maxim Guns and Hymn Books, and Trade-Gin and Torches of Progress and Enlightenment (patent adjustable ones, good to fire villages with, upon occasion), and balance the books, and arrive at the profit and loss, so that we may intelligently decide whether to continue the business or sell out the property and start a new Civilization Scheme on the proceeds?

Extending the Blessings of Civilization to our Brother who Sits in Darkness has been a good trade and has paid well, on the whole; and there is money in it yet, if carefully worked—but not enough, in my judgment, to make any considerable risk advisable. The People that Sit in Darkness are getting to be too scarce—too scarce and too shy. And such darkness as is now left is really of but an indifferent quality, and not dark enough for the game. The most of those People that Sit in Darkness have been furnished with more light than was good for them or profitable for us. We have been injudicious.

The Blessings-of-Civilization Trust, wisely and cautiously administered, is a Daisy. There is more money in it, more territory, more sovereignty, and other kinds of emolument, than there is in any other game that is played. But Christendom has been playing it badly of late years, and must certainly suffer by it, in my opinion. She has been so eager to get every stake that appeared on the green cloth, that the People who Sit in Darkness have noticed it—they have noticed it, and have begun to show alarm. They have become suspicious of the Blessings of Civilization. More—they have begun to examine them. This is not well. The Blessings of Civilization are all right, and a good commercial property; there could not be a better, in a dim light. In the right kind of a light, and at a proper distance, with the goods a little out of focus, they furnish this desirable exhibit to the Gentlemen who Sit in Darkness:

LOVE,	LAW AND ORDER,
JUSTICE,	LIBERTY,
GENTLENESS,	EQUALITY,
CHRISTIANITY,	HONORABLE DEALING,
PROTECTION TO THE WEAK,	MERCY,
TEMPERANCE,	EDUCATION,

—and so on.

There. Is it good? Sir, it is pie. It will bring into camp any idiot that sits in darkness anywhere. But not if we adulterate it. It is proper to be emphatic upon that point. This brand is strictly for Export—apparently. *Apparently.* Privately and confidentially, it is nothing of the kind. Privately and confidentially, it is merely an outside cover, gay and pretty and attractive, displaying the special patterns of our Civilization which we reserve for Home Consumption, while *inside* the bale is the Actual Thing that the Customer Sitting in Darkness buys with his blood and tears and land and liberty. That Actual Thing is, indeed, Civilization, but it is only for Export. Is there a difference between the two brands? In some of the details, yes.

We all know that the Business is being ruined. The reason is not far to seek. It is because our Mr. McKinley, and Mr. Chamberlain, and the Kaiser, and the Czar and the French have been exporting the Actual Thing *with the outside cover left off*. This is bad for the Game. It shows that these new players of it are not sufficiently acquainted with it.

It is a distress to look on and note the mismoves, they are so strange and so awkward. Mr. Chamberlain manufactures a war out of materials so inadequate and so fanciful that they make the boxes grieve and the gallery laugh, and he tries hard to persuade himself that it isn't purely a private raid for cash, but has a sort of dim, vague respectability about it somewhere, if he could only find the spot; and that, by and by, he can scour the flag clean again after he has finished dragging it through the mud, and make it shine and flash in the vault of heaven once more as it had shone and flashed there a thousand years in the world's respect until he laid his unfaithful hand upon it. It is bad play—bad. For it exposes the Actual Thing to Them that Sit in Darkness, and they say: "What! Christian against Christian? And only for money? Is *this* a case of magnanimity, forbearance, love, gentleness, mercy, protection of the weak—this strange and over-showy onslaught of an elephant upon a nest of field-mice, on the pretext that the mice had squeaked an insolence at him—conduct which 'no self-respecting government could allow to pass unavenged?' as Mr. Chamberlain said. Was that a good pretext in a small case, when it had not been a good pretext in a large one?—for only recently Russia had affronted the elephant three times and survived alive and unsmitten. Is this Civilization and Progress? Is it something better than we already possess? These harryings and burnings and desert-makings in the Transvaal—is this an improvement on our darkness? Is it, perhaps, possible that there are two kinds of Civilization—one for home consumption and one for the heathen market?"

Then They that Sit in Darkness are troubled, and shake their heads; and they read this extract from a letter of a British private, recounting his exploits in one of Methuen's victories, some days before the affair of Magersfontein, and they are troubled again:

> We tore up the hill and into the intrenchments, and the Boers saw we had them; so they dropped their guns and went down on their knees and put up their hands clasped, and begged for mercy. And we gave it them—*with the long spoon.*

The long spoon is the bayonet. See *Lloyd's Weekly*, London, of those days. The same number—and the same column—contained some quite unconscious satire in the form of shocked and bitter upbraidings of the Boers for their brutalities and inhumanities!

Next, to our heavy damage, the Kaiser went to playing the game without first mastering it. He lost a couple of missionaries in a riot in Shantung, and in his account he made an overcharge for them. China had to pay a hundred thousand dollars apiece for them, in money; twelve miles of territory, containing several millions of inhabitants and worth twenty million dollars; and to build a monument, and also a Christian church; whereas the people of China could have been depended upon to remember the missionaries without the help of these expensive memorials. This was all bad play. Bad, because it would not, and could not, and will not now or ever, deceive the Person Sitting in Darkness. He knows that it was an overcharge. He knows that a missionary is like any other man: he is worth merely what you can supply his place for, and no more. He is useful, but so is a doctor, so is a sheriff, so is an editor; but a just Emperor does not charge war-prices for such. A diligent, intelligent, but obscure missionary, and a diligent, intelligent country editor are worth much, and we know it; but they are not worth the earth. We esteem such an editor, and we are sorry to see him go; but when he goes, we should consider twelve miles of territory, and a church, and a fortune, over-compensation for his loss. I mean, if he was a Chinese editor, and we had to settle for him. It is no proper figure for an editor or a missionary; one can get shop-worn kings for less. It was bad play on the Kaiser's part. It got this property, true; but it *produced the Chinese revolt*, the indignant uprising of China's traduced patriots, the Boxers. The results have been expensive to Germany, and to the other Disseminators of Progress and the Blessings of Civilization.

The Kaiser's claim was paid, yet it was bad play, for it could not fail to have an evil effect upon Persons Sitting in Darkness in China. They would muse upon the event, and be likely to say: "Civilization is gracious and beautiful, for such is its reputation; but can we afford it? There are rich Chinamen, perhaps they could afford it; but this tax is not laid upon them, it is laid upon the peasants of Shantung; it is they that must pay this mighty sum, and their wages are but four cents a day. Is this a better civilization than ours, and holier and higher and nobler? Is not this rapacity? Is not this extortion? Would Germany charge America two hundred thousand dollars for two missionaries, and shake the mailed fist in her face, and send warships, and send soldiers, and say: 'Seize twelve miles of territory, worth twenty millions of dollars, as additional pay for the missionaries; and make those peasants build a monument to the missionaries, and a costly Christian church to remember them by?' And later would Germany say to her soldiers: 'March through America and slay, *giving no quarter;* make the German face there, as has been our Hun-face here, a terror for a thousand years; march through the Great Republic and slay, slay, slay, carving a road for our offended religion through its heart and bowels?' Would Germany do like this to America, to England, to France, to Russia? Or only to China the helpless—imitating the elephant's assault upon the field-mice? Had we better invest in this Civilization—this Civilization which called Napoleon a buccaneer for carrying off Venice's bronze horses, but which steals our ancient astronomical instruments from our walls, and goes looting like common bandits—that is, all the alien soldiers except America's; and (Americans again excepted) storms frightened villages and cables the result to glad journals at home every day: 'Chinese losses, 450 killed; ours, *one officer and two men wounded.* Shall proceed against neighboring village to-morrow, where a *massacre* is reported.' Can we afford Civilization?"

And, next, Russia must go and play the game injudiciously. She affronts England once or twice—with the Person Sitting in Darkness observing and noting; by moral assistance of France and Germany, she robs Japan of her hard-earned spoil, all swimming in Chinese blood—Port Arthur—with the Person again observing and noting; then she seizes Manchuria, raids its villages, and chokes its great river with the swollen corpses of countless massacred peasants—that astonished Person still observing and noting. And perhaps he is saying to himself: "It is yet *another* Civilized Power, with its banner of the Prince of Peace in one hand and its loot-basket and its butcher-knife in the other. Is there no salvation for us but to adopt Civilization and lift ourselves down to its level?"

And by and by comes America, and our Master of the Game plays it badly—plays it as Mr. Chamberláin was playing it in South Africa. It was a mistake to do that; also, it was one which was quite unlooked for in a Master who was playing it so well in Cuba. In Cuba, he was playing the usual and regular *American* game, and it was winning, for there is no way to beat it. The Master, contemplating Cuba, said: "Here is an oppressed and friendless little nation which is willing to fight to be free; we go partners, and put up the strength of seventy million sympathizers and the resources of the United States: play!" Nothing but Europe combined could call that hand: and Europe cannot combine on anything. There, in Cuba, he was following our great traditions in a way which made us very proud of him, and proud of the deep dissatisfaction which his play was provoking in Continental Europe. Moved by a high inspiration, he threw out those stirring words which proclaimed that forcible annexation would be "criminal aggression;" and in that utterance fired another "shot heard round the world." The memory of that fine saying will be outlived by the remembrance of no act of his but one —that he forgot it within the twelvemonth, and its honorable gospel along with it.

For, presently, came the Philippine temptation. It was strong; it was too strong, and he made that bad mistake: he played the European game, the Chamberlain game. It was a pity; it was a great pity, that error; that one grievous error, that irrevocable error. For it was the very place and time to play the American game again. And at no cost. Rich winnings to be gathered in, too; rich and permanent; indestructible; a fortune transmissible forever to the children of the flag. Not land, not money, not dominion—no, something worth many times more than that dross: our share, the spectacle of a nation of long harassed and persecuted slaves set free through our influence; our posterity's share, the golden memory of that fair deed. The game was in our hands. If it had been played according to the American rules, Dewey would have sailed away from Manila as soon as he had destroyed the Spanish fleet—after putting up a sign on shore guaranteeing foreign property and life against damage by the Filipinos, and warning the Powers that interference with the emancipated patriots would be regarded as an act unfriendly to the United States. The Powers cannot combine, in even a bad cause, and the sign would not have been molested.

Dewey could have gone about his affairs elsewhere, and left the competent Filipino army to starve out the little Spanish garrison and send it home, and the Filipino citizens to set up the form of government they might prefer, and deal with the friars and their doubtful acquisitions according to Filipino ideas of fairness and justice—ideas which have since been tested and found to be of as high an order as any that prevail in Europe or America.

But we played the Chamberlain game, and lost the chance to add another Cuba and another honorable deed to our good record.

The more we examine the mistake, the more clearly we perceive that it is going to be bad for the Business. The Person Sitting in Darkness is almost sure to say: "There is something curious about this—curious and unaccountable. There must be two Americas: one that sets the captive free, and one that takes a once-captive's new freedom away from him and picks a quarrel with him with nothing to found it on; then kills him to get his land."

The truth is, the Person Sitting in Darkness *is* saying things like that; and for the sake of the Business we must persuade him to look at the Philippine matter in another and healthier way. We must arrange his opinions for him. I believe it can be done; for Mr. Chamberlain has arranged England's opinion of the South African matter, and done it most cleverly and successfully. He presented the facts—some of the facts—and showed those confiding people what the facts meant. He did it statistically, which is a good way. He used the formula: "Twice 2 are 14, and 2 from 9 leaves 35." Figures are effective; figures will convince the elect.

Now, my plan is a still bolder one than Mr. Chamberlain's, though apparently a copy of it. Let us be franker than Mr. Chamberlain; let us audaciously present the whole of the facts, shirking none, then explain them according to Mr. Chamberlain's formula. This daring truthfulness will astonish and dazzle the Person Sitting in Darkness, and he will take the Explanation down before his mental vision has had time to get back into focus. Let us say to him:

"Our case is simple. On the 1st of May, Dewey destroyed the Spanish fleet. This left the Archipelago in the hands of its proper and rightful owners, the Filipino nation. Their army numbered 30,000 men, and they were competent to whip out or starve out the little Spanish garrison; then the people could set up a government of their own devising. Our traditions required that Dewey should now set up his warning sign, and go away. But the Master of the Game happened to think of another plan—the European plan. He acted upon it. This was, to send out an army—ostensibly to help the native patriots put the finishing touch upon their long and plucky struggle for independence, but really to take their land away from them and keep it. That is, in the interest of Progress and Civilization. The plan developed, stage by stage, and quite satisfactorily. We entered into a military alliance with the trusting Filipinos, and they hemmed in Manila on the land side, and by their valuable help the place, with its garrison of 8,000 or 10,000 Spaniards, was captured—a thing which we could not have accomplished unaided at that time. We got their help by—by ingenuity. We knew they were fighting for their independence, and that they had been at it for two years. We knew they supposed that we also were fighting in their worthy cause—just as we had helped the Cubans fight for Cuban independence—and we allowed them to go on thinking so. *Until Manila was ours and we could get along without them.* Then we showed our hand. Of course, they were surprised—that was natural; surprised and disappointed; disappointed and grieved. To them it looked unAmerican; uncharacteristic; foreign to our established traditions. And this was natural, too; for we were only playing the American Game in public—in private it was the European. It was neatly done, very neatly, and it bewildered them. They could not understand it; for we had been so friendly—so affectionate, even—with those simple-minded patriots! We, our own selves, had brought back out of exile their leader, their hero, their hope, their Washington—Aguinaldo; brought him in a warship, in high honor, under the sacred shelter and hospitality of the flag; brought him back and restored him to his people, and got their moving and eloquent gratitude for it. Yes, we had been so friendly to them, and had heartened them up in so many ways! We had lent them guns and ammunition; advised with them; exchanged pleasant courtesies with them; placed our sick and wounded in their kindly care; entrusted our Spanish prisoners to their humane and honest hands; fought shoulder to shoulder with them against 'the common enemy' (our own phrase); praised their courage, praised their gallantry, praised their mercifulness, praised their fine and honorable conduct; borrowed their trenches, borrowed strong positions which they had previously captured from the Spaniard; petted them, lied to them—officially proclaiming that our land and naval forces came to give them their freedom and displace the bad Spanish Government—fooled them, used them until we needed them no longer; then derided the sucked orange and threw it away. We kept the positions which we had beguiled them of; by and by, we moved a force forward and overlapped patriot ground—a clever thought, for we needed trouble, and this would produce it. A Filipino soldier, crossing the ground, where no one had a right to forbid him, was shot by our sentry. The badgered patriots resented this with arms, without waiting to know whether Aguinaldo, who was absent, would approve or not. Aguinaldo did not approve; but that availed nothing. What we wanted, in the interest of Progress and Civilization, was the Archipelago, unencumbered by patriots struggling for independence; and War was what we needed. We clinched our opportunity. It is Mr. Chamberlain's case over again—at least in its motive and intention; and we played the game as adroitly as he played it himself."

At this point in our frank statement of fact to the Person Sitting in Darkness, we should throw in a little trade-taffy about the Blessings of Civilization—for a change, and for the refreshment of his spirit—then go on with our tale:

"We and the patriots having captured Manila, Spain's ownership of the Archipelago and her sovereignty over it were at an end—obliterated—annihilated—not a rag or shred of either remaining behind. It was then that we conceived the divinely humorous idea of *buying* both of these spectres from Spain! [It is quite safe to confess this to the Person Sitting in

Darkness, since neither he nor any other sane person will believe it.] In buying those ghosts for twenty millions, we also contracted to take care of the friars and their accumulations. I think we also agreed to propagate leprosy and smallpox, but as to this there is doubt. But it is not important; persons afflicted with the friars do not mind other diseases.

"With our Treaty ratified, Manila subdued, and our Ghosts secured, we had no further use for Aguinaldo and the owners of the Archipelago. We forced a war, and we have been hunting America's guest and ally through the woods and swamps ever since."

At this point in the tale, it will be well to boast a little of our war-work and our heroisms in the field, so as to make our performance look as fine as England's in South Africa; but I believe it will not be best to emphasize this too much. We must be cautious. Of course, we must read the war-telegrams to the Person, in order to keep up our frankness; but we can throw an air of humorousness over them, and that will modify their grim eloquence a little, and their rather indiscreet exhibitions of gory exultation. Before reading to him the following display heads of the dispatches of November 18, 1900, it will be well to practice on them in private first, so as to get the right tang of lightness and gaiety into them:

"ADMINISTRATION WEARY OF PROTRACTED HOSTILITIES!"
"REAL WAR AHEAD FOR FILIPINO REBELS" *
"WILL SHOW NO MERCY!"
"KITCHENER'S PLAN ADOPTED!"

* "Rebels!" Mumble that funny word—don't let the Person catch it distinctly. (M.T.)

Kitchener knows how to handle disagreeable people who are fighting for their homes and their liberties, and we must let on that we are merely imitating Kitchener, and have no national interest in the matter, further than to get ourselves admired by the Great Family of Nations, in which august company our Master of the Game has bought a place for us in the back row.

Of course, we must not venture to ignore our General MacArthur's reports—oh, why do they keep on printing those embarrassing things?—we must drop them trippingly from the tongue and take the chances:

> During the last ten months our losses have been 268 killed and 750 wounded; Filipino loss, *three thousand two hundred and twenty-seven killed,* and 694 wounded.

We must stand ready to grab the Person Sitting in Darkness, for he will swoon away at this confession, saying: "Good God, those 'niggers' spare their wounded, and the Americans massacre theirs!"

We must bring him to, and coax him and coddle him, and assure him that the ways of Providence are best, and that it would not become us to find fault with them; and then, to show him that we are only imitators, not originators, we must read the following passage from the letter of an American soldier-lad in the Philippines to his mother, published in *Public Opinion,* of Decorah, Iowa, describing the finish of a victorious battle:

> "WE NEVER LEFT ONE ALIVE. IF ONE WAS WOUNDED, WE WOULD RUN OUR BAYONETS THROUGH HIM."

Having now laid all the historical facts before the Person Sitting in Darkness, we should bring him to again, and explain them to him. We should say to him:

"They look doubtful, but in reality they are not. There have been lies; yes, but they were told in a good cause. We have been treacherous; but that was only in order that real good might come out of apparent evil. True, we have crushed a deceived and confiding people; we have turned against the weak and the friendless who trusted us; we have stamped out a just and intelligent and well-ordered republic; we have stabbed an ally in the back and slapped the face of a guest; we have bought a Shadow from an enemy that hadn't it to sell; we have robbed a trusting friend of his land and his liberty; we have invited our clean young men to shoulder a discredited musket and do bandit's work under a flag which bandits have been accustomed to fear, not to follow; we have debauched America's honor and blackened her face before the world; but each detail was for the best. We know this. The Head of every State and Sovereignty in Christendom and ninety per cent of every legislative body in Christendom, including our Congress and our fifty State Legislatures, are members not only of the church, but also of the Blessings-of-Civilization Trust. This world-girdling accumulation of trained morals, high principles, and justice, cannot do an unright thing, an unfair thing, an ungenerous thing, an unclean thing. It knows what it is about. Give yourself no uneasiness; it is all right."

Now then, that will convince the Person. You will see. It will restore the Business. Also, it will elect the

Master of the Game to the vacant place in the Trinity of our national gods; and there on their high thrones the Three will sit, age after age, in the people's sight, each bearing the Emblem of his service: Washington, the Sword of the Liberator; Lincoln, the Slave's Broken Chains; the Master, the Chains Repaired.

It will give the Business a splendid new start. You will see.

Everything is prosperous, now; everything is just as we should wish it. We have got the Archipelago, and we shall never give it up. Also, we have every reason to hope that we shall have an opportunity before very long to slip out of our Congressional contract with Cuba and give her something better in the place of it. It is a rich country, and many of us are already beginning to see that the contract was a sentimental mistake. But now—right now—is the best time to do some profitable rehabilitating work—work that will set us up and make us comfortable, and discourage gossip. We cannot conceal from ourselves that, privately, we are a little troubled about our uniform. It is one of our prides; it is acquainted with honor; it is familiar with great deeds and noble; we love it, we revere it; and so this errand it is on makes us uneasy. And our flag—another pride of ours, our chiefest! We have worshipped it so; and when we have seen it in far lands—glimpsing it unexpectedly in that strange sky, waving its welcome and benediction to us—we have caught our breath, and uncovered our heads, and couldn't speak, for a moment, for the thought of what it was to us and the great ideals it stood for. Indeed, we *must* do something about these things; we must not have the flag out there, and the uniform. They are not needed there; we can manage in some other way. England manages, as regards the uniform, and so can we. We have to send soldiers—we can't get out of that—but we can disguise them. It is the way England does in South Africa. Even Mr. Chamberlain himself takes pride in England's honorable uniform, and makes the army down there wear an ugly and odious and appropriate disguise, of yellow stuff such as quarantine flags are made of, and which are hoisted to warn the healthy away from unclean disease and repulsive death. This cloth is called khaki. We could adopt it. It is light, comfortable, grotesque, and deceives the enemy, for he cannot conceive of a soldier being concealed in it.

And as for a flag for the Philippine Province, it is easily managed. We can have a special one—our States do it: we can have just our usual flag, with the white stripes painted black and the stars replaced by the skull and cross-bones.

And we do not need that Civil Commission out there. Having no powers, it has to invent them, and that kind of work cannot be effectively done by just anybody; an expert is required. Mr. Croker can be spared. We do not want the United States represented there, but only the Game.

By help of these suggested amendments, Progress and Civilization in that country can have a boom, and it will take in the Persons who are Sitting in Darkness, and we can resume Business at the old stand.

Grief and Mourning for the Night (1906)

This incident burst upon the world last Friday in an official cablegram from the commander of our forces in the Philippines to our Government at Washington. The substance of it was as follows:

A tribe of Moros, dark skinned savages, had fortified themselves in the bowl of an extinct crater not many miles from Jolo; and as they were hostiles, and bitter against us because we have been trying for eight years to take their liberties away from them, their presence in that position was a menace. Our commander, General Leonard Wood, ordered a reconnaissance. It was found that the Moros numbered six hundred, counting women and children; that their crater bowl was in the summit of a peak or mountain twenty-two hundred feet above sea level, and very difficult of access for Christian troops and artillery. Then General Wood ordered a surprise, and went along himself to see the order carried out. Our troops climbed the heights by devious and difficult trails, and even took some artillery with them. The kind of artillery is not specified, but in one place it was hoisted up a sharp acclivity by tackle a distance of some three hundred feet. Arrived at the rim of the crater, the battle began. Our soldiers numbered five hundred and forty. They were assisted by auxiliaries consisting of a detachment of native constabulary in our pay—their numbers not given—and by a naval detachment, whose numbers are not stated. But apparently the contending parties were about equal as to number—six hundred men on our side, on the edge of the bowl; six hundred men, women and children in the bottom of the bowl. Depth of the bowl, 50 feet.

General Wood's order was "Kill or capture the six hundred."

The battle began—it is officially called by that name—our forces firing down into the crater with their artillery and their deadly small arms of precision; the savages furiously returning the fire, probably with brickbats—though this is merely a surmise of mine, as the weapons used by the savages are not nominated in the cablegram. Heretofore the Moros have used knives and clubs mainly; also ineffectual trade-muskets when they had any.

The official report stated that the battle was fought with prodigious energy on both sides during a day and a half, and that it ended with a complete victory for the American arms. The completeness of the victory is established by this fact: that of the six hundred Moros not one was left alive. The brilliancy of the victory is established by this other fact, to wit: that of our six hundred heroes only fifteen lost their lives.

General Wood was present and looking on. His order had been "Kill *or* capture those savages." Apparently our little army considered that the "or" left them authorized to kill *or* capture according to taste, and that their taste had remained what it has been for eight years, in our army out there—the taste of Christian butchers.

The official report quite properly extolled and magnified the "heroism" and "gallantry" of our troops; lamented the loss of the fifteen who perished, and elaborated the wounds of thirty-two of our men who suffered injury, and even minutely and faithfully described the nature of the wounds, in the interest of future historians of the United States. It mentioned that a private had one of his elbows scraped by a missile, and the private's name was mentioned. Another private had the end of his nose scraped by a missile. His name was also mentioned—by cable, at one dollar and fifty cents a word.

Next day's news confirmed the previous day's report and named our fifteen killed and thirty-two wounded *again,* and once more described the wounds and gilded them with the right adjectives.

Let us now consider two or three details of our military history. In one of the great battles of the civil war ten per cent. of the forces engaged on the two sides were killed and wounded. At Waterloo, where four hundred thousand men were present on the two sides, fifty thousand fell, killed and wounded, in five hours, leaving three hundred and fifty thousand sound and all right for further adventures. Eight years ago, when the pathetic comedy called the Cuban war was played, we summoned two hundred and fifty thousand men. We fought a number of showy battles, and when the war was over we had lost two hundred and sixty-eight men out of our two hundred and fifty thousand, in killed and wounded in the field, and just *fourteen times as many* by the gallantry of the army doctors in the hospitals and camps. We did not exterminate the Spaniards—

far from it. In each engagement we left an average of *two per cent.* of the enemy killed or crippled on the field.

Contrast these things with the great statistics which have arrived from that Moro crater! There, with six hundred engaged on each side, we lost fifteen men killed outright, and we had thirty-two wounded—counting that nose and that elbow. The enemy numbered six hundred—including women and children—and we abolished them utterly, leaving not even a baby alive to cry for its dead mother. *This is incomparably the greatest victory that was ever achieved by the Christian soldiers of the United States.*

Now then, how has it been received? The splendid news appeared with splendid display-heads in every newspaper in this city of four million and thirteen thousand inhabitants, on Friday morning. But there was not a single reference to it in the editorial columns of any one of those newspapers. The news appeared again in all the evening papers of Friday, and again those papers were editorially silent upon our vast achievement. Next day's additional statistics and particulars appeared in all the morning papers, and still without a line of editorial rejoicing or a mention of the matter in any way. These additions appeared in the evening papers of that same day (Saturday) and again without a word of comment. In the columns devoted to correspondence, in the morning and evening papers of Friday and Saturday, nobody said a word about the "battle." Ordinarily those columns are teeming with the passions of the citizen; he lets no incident go by, whether it be large or small, without pouring out his praise or blame, his joy or his indignation about the matter in the correspondence column. But, as I have said, during those two days he was as silent as the editors themselves. So far as I can find out, there was only one person among our eighty millions who allowed himself the privilege of a public remark on this great occasion—that was the President of the United States. All day Friday he was as studiously silent as the rest. But on Saturday he recognized that his duty required him to say something, and he took his pen and performed that duty. If I know President Roosevelt—and I am sure I do—this utterance cost him more pain and shame than any other that ever issued from his pen or his mouth. I am far from blaming him. If I had been in his place my official duty would have compelled me to say what he said. It was a convention, an old tradition, and he had to be loyal to it. There was no help for it. This is what he said:

Washington, March 10

WOOD, *Manila:*—

I congratulate you and the officers and men of your command upon the brilliant feat of arms wherein you and they so well upheld the honor of the American flag.

(Signed) THEODORE ROOSEVELT

His whole utterance is merely a convention. Not a word of what he said came out of his heart. He knew perfectly well that to pen six hundred helpless and weaponless savages in a hole like rats in a trap and massacre them in detail during a stretch of a day and a half, from a safe position on the heights above, was no brilliant feat of arms—and would not have been a brilliant feat of arms even if Christian America represented by its salaried soldiers, had shot them down with Bibles and the Golden Rule instead of bullets. He knew perfectly well that our uniformed assassins had *not* upheld the honor of the American flag, but had done as they have been doing continuously for eight years in the Philippines—that is to say, they had dishonored it.

The next day, Sunday,—which was yesterday—the cable brought us additional news—still more splendid news—still more honor for the flag. The first display-head shouts this information at us in stentorian capitals: "WOMEN SLAIN IN MORO SLAUGHTER."

"Slaughter" is a good word. Certainly there is not a better one in the Unabridged Dictionary for this occasion.

The next display line says:

"With Children They Mixed in Mob in Crater, and All Died Together."

They were mere naked savages, and yet there is a sort of pathos about it when that word children falls under your eye, for it always brings before us our perfectest symbol of innocence and helplessness; and by help of its deathless eloquence color, creed and nationality vanish away and we see only that they are children—merely children. And if they are frightened and crying and in trouble, our pity goes out to them by natural impulse. We see a picture. We see the small forms. We see the terrified faces. We see the tears. We see the small hands clinging in supplication to the mother; but we do not see those children that we are speaking about. We see in their places the little creatures whom we know and love.

The next heading blazes with American and Christian glory like to the sun in the zenith:

"Death List is Now 900."

I was never so enthusiastically proud of the flag till now!

The next heading explains how safely our daring soldiers were located. It says:

"Impossible to Tell Sexes Apart in Fierce Battle on Top of Mount Dajo."

The naked savages were so far away, down in the bottom of that trap, that our soldiers could not tell the breasts of a woman from the rudimentary paps of a man—so far away that they couldn't tell a toddling little child from a black six-footer. *This was by all odds the least dangerous battle that Christian soldiers of any nationality were ever engaged in.*

The next heading says:

"Fighting for Four Days."

So our men were at it four days instead of a day and a half. It was a long and happy picnic with nothing to do but sit in comfort and fire the Golden Rule into those people down there and imagine letters to write home to the admiring families, and pile glory upon glory. Those savages fighting for their liberties had the four days too, but it must have been a sorrowful time for them. Every day they saw two hundred and twenty-five of their number slain, and this provided them grief and mourning for the night—and doubtless without even the relief and consolation of knowing that in the meantime they had slain four of their enemies and wounded some more on the elbow and the nose.

The closing heading says:

"Lieutenant Johnson Blown from Parapet by Exploding Artillery Gallantly Leading Charge."

Lieutenant Johnson has pervaded the cablegrams from the first. He and his wound have sparkled around through them like the serpentine thread of fire that goes excursioning through the black crisp fabric of a fragment of burnt paper. It reminds one of Gillette's comedy farce of a few years ago, "Too Much Johnson." Apparently Johnson was the only wounded man on our side whose wound was worth anything as an advertisement. It has made a great deal more noise in the world than has any similar event since "Humpty Dumpty" fell off the wall and got injured. The official despatches do not know which to admire most, Johnson's adorable wound or the nine hundred murders. The ecstasies flowing from Army Headquarters on the other side of the globe to the White House, at one dollar and a half a word, have set fire to similar ecstasies in the President's breast. It appears that the immortally wounded was a Rough Rider under Lieutenant Colonel Theodore Roosevelt at San Juan Hill—that twin of Waterloo—when the Colonel of the regiment, the present Major General Dr. Leonard Wood, went to the rear to bring up the pills and missed the fight. The President has a warm place in his heart for anybody who was present at that bloody collision of military solar systems, and so he lost no time in cabling to the wounded hero "How are you?" And got a cable answer, "Fine, thanks." This is historical. This will go down to posterity.

Johnson was wounded in the shoulder with a slug.

The slug was in a shell—for the account says the damage was caused by an exploding shell which blew Johnson off the rim. The people down in the hole had no artillery; therefore it was our artillery that blew Johnson off the rim. And so it is now a matter of historical record that the only officer of ours who acquired a wound of advertising dimensions got it at our hands, not the enemy's. It seems more than probable that if we had placed our soldiers out of the way of our own weapons, we should have come out of the most extraordinary battle in all history without a scratch. . . .

The ominous paralysis continues. There has been a slight sprinkle—an exceedingly slight sprinkle—in the correspondence columns, of angry rebukes of the President for calling this cowardly massacre a "brilliant feat of arms" and for praising our butchers for "holding up the honor of the flag" in that singular way; but there is hardly a ghost of a whisper about the feat of arms in the editorial columns of the papers.

I hope that this silence will continue. It is about as eloquent and as damaging and effective as the most indignant words could be, I think. When a man is sleeping in a noise, his sleep goes placidly on; but if the noise stops, the stillness wakes him. This silence has continued five days now. Surely it must be waking the drowsy nation. Surely the nation must be wondering what it means. A five-day silence following a world-astonishing event has not happened on this planet since the daily newspaper was invented.

At a luncheon party of men convened yesterday to

God-speed George Harvey, who is leaving to-day for a vacation in Europe, all the talk was about the brilliant feat of arms; and no one had anything to say about it that either the President or Major General Dr. Wood or the damaged Johnson would regard as complimentary, or as proper comment to put into our histories. Harvey said he believed that the shock and shame of this episode would eat down deeper and deeper into the hearts of the nation and fester there and produce results. He believed it would destroy the Republican party and President Roosevelt. I cannot believe that the prediction will come true, for the reason that prophecies which promise valuable things, desirable things, good things, worthy things, never come true. Prophecies of this kind are like wars fought in a good cause—they are so rare that they don't count.

The War-Prayer
(1904–1905)

It was a time of great and exalting excitement. The country was up in arms, the war was on, in every breast burned the holy fire of patriotism; the drums were beating, the bands playing, the toy pistols popping, the bunched firecrackers hissing and spluttering; on every hand and far down the receding and fading spread of roofs and balconies a fluttering wilderness of flags flashed in the sun; daily the young volunteers marched down the wide avenue gay and fine in their new uniforms, the proud fathers and mothers and sisters and sweethearts cheering them with voices choked with happy emotion as they swung by; nightly the packed mass-meetings listened, panting, to patriot oratory which stirred the deepest deeps of their hearts, and which they interrupted at briefest intervals with cyclones of applause, the tears running down their cheeks the while; in the churches the pastors preached devotion to flag and country, and invoked the God of Battles, beseeching His aid in our good cause in outpourings of fervid eloquence which moved every listener. It was indeed a glad and gracious time, and the half dozen rash spirits that ventured to disapprove of the war and cast a doubt upon its righteousness straightway got such a stern and angry warning that for their personal safety's sake they quickly shrank out of sight and offended no more in that way.

Sunday morning came—next day the battalions would leave for the front; the church was filled; the volunteers were there, their young faces alight with martial dreams—visions of the stern advance, the gathering momentum, the rushing charge, the flashing sabres, the flight of the foe, the tumult, the enveloping smoke, the fierce pursuit, the surrender!—then home from the war, bronzed heroes, welcomed, adored, submerged in golden seas of glory! With the volunteers sat their dear ones, proud, happy, and envied by the neighbors and friends who had no sons and brothers to send forth to the field of honor, there to win for the flag, or, failing, die the noblest of noble deaths. The service proceeded; a war-chapter from the Old Testament was read; the first prayer was said; it was followed by an organ-burst that shook the building, and with one impulse the house rose, with glowing eyes and beating hearts and poured out that tremendous invocation—

> God the all-terrible! Thou who ordainest,
> Thunder thy clarion and lightning thy sword!

Then came the "long" prayer. None could remember the like of it for passionate pleading and moving and beautiful language. The burden of its supplication was, that the ever-merciful and benignant Father of us all would watch over our noble young soldiers, and aid, comfort, and encourage them in their patriotic work; bless them, shield them in the day of battle and the hour of peril, bear them in His mighty hand, make them strong and confident, invincible in the bloody onset, help them to crush the foe, grant to them and to their flag and country imperishable honor and glory—

An aged stranger entered, and moved with slow and noiseless step up the main aisle, his eyes fixed upon the minister, his long body clothed in a robe that reached to his feet, his head bare, his white hair descending in a frothy cataract to his shoulders, his seamy face unnaturally pale, pale even to ghastliness. With all eyes following him and wondering, he made his silent way; without pausing, he ascended to the preacher's side and stood there, waiting. With shut lids the preacher, unconscious of his presence, continued his moving prayer, and at last finished it with the words, uttered in fervent appeal, "Bless our arms, grant us the victory, O Lord our God, Father and Protector of our land and flag!"

The stranger touched his arm, motioned him to step aside—which the startled minister did—and took his place. During some moments he surveyed the spell-bound audience with solemn eyes, in which burned an uncanny light; then in a deep voice he said—

"I come from the Throne—bearing a message from Almighty God!" The words smote the house with a shock; if the stranger perceived it he gave it no attention. "He has heard the prayer of His servant your shepherd, and will grant it if such shall be your desire after I, His messenger, shall have explained to you its import—that is to say, its full import. For it is like unto many of the prayers of men, in that it asks for more than he who utters it is aware of—except he pause and think.

"God's servant and yours has prayed his prayer.

Has he paused, and taken thought? Is it one prayer? No, it is two—one uttered, the other not. Both have reached the ear of Him who heareth all supplications, the spoken and the unspoken. Ponder this—keep it in mind. If you would beseech a blessing upon yourself, beware! lest without intent you invoke a curse upon a neighbor at the same time. If you pray for the blessing of rain upon your crop which needs it, by that act you are possibly praying for a curse upon some neighbor's crop which may not need rain and can be injured by it.

"You have heard your servant's prayer—the uttered part of it. I am commissioned of God to put into words the other part of it—that part which the pastor—and also you in your hearts—fervently prayed silently. And ignorantly and unthinkingly? God grant that it was so! You heard these words: 'Grant us the victory, O Lord our God!' That is sufficient. The *whole* of the uttered prayer is compacted into those pregnant words. Elaborations were not necessary. When you have prayed for victory you have prayed for many unmentioned results which follow victory—*must* follow it, cannot help but follow it. Upon the listening spirit of God the Father fell also the unspoken part of the prayer. He commandeth me to put it into words. Listen!

"O Lord, our Father, our young patriots, idols of our hearts, go forth to battle—be Thou near them! With them—in spirit—we also go forth from the sweet peace of our beloved firesides to smite the foe. O Lord, our God, help us to tear their soldiers to bloody shreds with our shells; help us to cover their smiling fields with the pale forms of their patriot dead; help us to drown the thunder of the guns with the shrieks of their wounded, writhing in pain; help us to lay waste their humble homes with a hurricane of fire; help us to wring the hearts of their unoffending widows with unavailing grief; help us to turn them out roofless with their little children to wander unfriended the wastes of their desolated land in rags and hunger and thirst, sport of the sun-flames of summer and the icy winds of winter, broken in spirit, worn with travail, imploring Thee for the refuge of the grave and denied it—for our sakes who adore Thee, Lord, blast their hopes, blight their lives, protract their bitter pilgrimage, make heavy their steps, water their way with their tears, stain the white snow with the blood of their wounded feet! We ask it, in the spirit of love, of Him Who is the Source of Love, and Who is the ever-faithful refuge and friend of all that are sore beset and seek His aid with humble and contrite hearts. Amen."

[*After a pause.*] "Ye have prayed it; if ye still desire it, speak!—The messenger of the Most High waits."

It was believed afterwards, that the man was a lunatic, because there was no sense in what he said.

The Human Condition

Man is the Reasoning Animal. Such is the claim. I think it is open to dispute. Indeed, my experiments have proven to me that he is the Unreasoning Animal. Note his history. . . . It seems plain to me that whatever he is he is not a reasoning animal. His record is the fantastic record of a maniac. I consider that the strongest count against his intelligence is the fact that with that record back of him he blandly sets himself up as the head animal of the lot: whereas by his own standards he is the bottom one.

—*From "The Lowest Animal"* (*1897?*)

The Great Revolution in Pitcairn (1897)

Let me refresh the reader's memory a little. Nearly a hundred years ago the crew of the British ship Bounty mutinied, set the captain and his officers adrift upon the open sea, took possession of the ship, and sailed southward. They procured wives for themselves among the natives of Tahiti, then proceeded to a lonely little rock in mid-Pacific, called Pitcairn's Island, wrecked the vessel, stripped her of everything that might be useful to a new colony, and established themselves on shore.

Pitcairn's is so far removed from the track of commerce that it was many years before another vessel touched there. It had always been considered an uninhabited island; so when a ship did at last drop its anchor there, in 1808, the captain was greatly surprised to find the place peopled. Although the mutineers had fought among themselves, and gradually killed each other off until only two or three of the original stock remained, these tragedies had not occurred before a number of children had been born; so in 1808 the island had a population of twenty-seven persons. John Adams, the chief mutineer, still survived, and was to live many years yet, as governor and patriarch of the flock. From being mutineer and homicide, he had turned Christian and teacher, and his nation of twenty-seven persons was now the purest and devoutest in Christendom. Adams had long ago hoisted the British flag and constituted his island an appanage of the British crown.

To-day the population numbers ninety persons,—sixteen men, nineteen women, twenty-five boys, and thirty girls,—all descendants of the mutineers, all bearing the family names of those mutineers, and all speaking English, and English only. The island stands high up out of the sea, and has precipitous walls. It is about three quarters of a mile long, and in places is as much as half a mile wide. Such arable land as it affords is held by the several families, according to a division made many years ago. There is some live stock,—goats, pigs, chickens, and cats; but no dogs, and no large animals. There is one church building,—used also as a capitol, a schoolhouse, and a public library. The title of the governor has been, for a generation or two, "Magistrate and Chief Ruler, in subordination to her Majesty the Queen of Great Britain." It was his province to *make* the laws, as well as execute them. His office was elective; everybody over seventeen years old had a vote,—no matter about the sex.

The sole occupations of the people were farming and fishing; their sole recreation, religious services. There has never been a shop in the island, nor any money. The habits and dress of the people have always been primitive, and their laws simple to puerility. They have lived in a deep Sabbath tranquillity, far from the world and its ambitions and vexations, and neither knowing nor caring what was going on in the mighty empires that lie beyond their limitless ocean solitudes. Once in three or four years a ship touched there, moved them with aged news of bloody battles, devastating epidemics, fallen thrones, and ruined dynasties, then traded them some soap and flannel for some yams and bread-fruit, and sailed away, leaving them to retire into their peaceful dreams and pious dissipations once more.

On the 8th of last September, Admiral de Horsey, commander-in-chief of the British fleet in the Pacific, visited Pitcairn's Island, and speaks as follows in his official report to the admiralty:—

"They have beans, carrots, turnips, cabbages, and a little maize; pineapples, fig-trees, custard apples, and oranges; lemons and cocoa-nuts. Clothing is obtained alone from passing ships, in barter for refreshments. There are no springs on the island, but as it rains generally once a month they have plenty of water, although at times, in former years, they have suffered from drought. No alcoholic liquors, except for medicinal purposes, are used, and a drunkard is unknown. . . .

"The necessary articles required by the islanders are best shown by those we furnished in barter for refreshments: namely, flannel, serge, drill, half-boots, combs, tobacco, and soap. They also stand much in need of maps and slates for their school, and tools of any kind are most acceptable. I caused them to be supplied from the public stores with a union-jack for display on the arrival of ships, and a pit saw, of which they were greatly in need. This, I trust, will meet the approval of their lordships. If the munificent people of England were only aware of the wants of this most deserving little colony, they would not long go unsupplied. . . .

"Divine service is held every Sunday at 10.30 A.M.

and at 3 P.M., in the house built and used by John Adams for that purpose until he died in 1829. It is conducted strictly in accordance with the liturgy of the Church of England, by Mr. Simon Young, their selected pastor, who is much respected. A Bible class is held every Wednesday, when all who conveniently can attend. There is also a general meeting for prayer on the first Friday in every month. Family prayers are said in every house the first thing in the morning and the last thing in the evening, and no food is partaken of without asking God's blessing before and afterwards. Of these islanders' religious attributes no one can speak without deep respect. A people whose greatest pleasure and privilege is to commune in prayer with their God, and to join in hymns of praise, and who are, moreover, cheerful, diligent, and probably freer from vice than any other community, need no priest among them."

Now I come to a sentence in the admiral's report which he dropped carelessly from his pen, no doubt, and never gave the matter a second thought. He little imagined what a freight of tragic prophecy it bore! This is the sentence:

"One stranger, an American, has settled on the island,—*a doubtful acquisition.*"

A doubtful acquisition indeed! Captain Ormsby, in the American ship Hornet, touched at Pitcairn's nearly four months after the admiral's visit, and from the facts which he gathered there we now know all about that American. Let us put these facts together, in historical form. The American's name was Butterworth Stavely. As soon as he had become well acquainted with all the people,—and this took but a few days, of course,—he began to ingratiate himself with them by all the arts he could command. He became exceedingly popular, and much looked up to; for one of the first things he did was to forsake his worldly way of life, and throw all his energies into religion. He was always reading his Bible, or praying, or singing hymns, or asking blessings. In prayer, no one had such "liberty" as he, no one could pray so long or so well.

At last, when he considered the time to be ripe, he began secretly to sow the seeds of discontent among the people. It was his deliberate purpose, from the beginning, to subvert the government, but of course he kept that to himself for a time. He used different arts with different individuals. He awakened dissatisfaction in one quarter by calling attention to the shortness of the Sunday services; he argued that there should be three three-hour services on Sunday instead of only two. Many had secretly held this opinion before; they now privately banded themselves into a party to work for it. He showed certain of the women that they were not allowed sufficient voice in the prayer-meetings; thus another party was formed. No weapon was beneath his notice; he even descended to the children, and awoke discontent in their breasts because—as *he* discovered for them—they had not enough Sunday-school. This created a third party.

Now, as the chief of these parties, he found himself the strongest power in the community. So he proceeded to his next move,—a no less important one than the impeachment of the chief magistrate, James Russell Nickoy; a man of character and ability, and possessed of great wealth, he being the owner of a house with a parlor to it, three acres and a half of yam land, and the only boat in Pitcairn's, a whale-boat; and, most unfortunately, a pretext for this impeachment offered itself at just the right time. One of the earliest and most precious laws of the island was the law against trespass. It was held in great reverence, and was regarded as the palladium of the people's liberties. About thirty years ago an important case came before the courts under this law, in this wise: a chicken belonging to Elizabeth Young (aged, at that time, fifty-eight, a daughter of John Mills, one of the mutineers of the Bounty) trespassed upon the grounds of Thursday October Christian (aged twenty-nine, a grandson of Fletcher Christian, one of the mutineers). Christian killed the chicken. According to the law, Christian could keep the chicken; or, if he preferred, he could restore its remains to the owner, and receive damages in "produce" to an amount equivalent to the waste and injury wrought by the trespasser. The court records set forth that "the said Christian aforesaid did deliver the aforesaid remains to the said Elizabeth Young, and did demand one bushel of Yams in satisfaction of the damage done." But Elizabeth Young considered the demand exorbitant; the parties could not agree; therefore Christian brought suit in the courts. He lost his case in the justice's court; at least, he was awarded only a half peck of yams, which he considered insufficient, and in the nature of a defeat. He appealed. The case lingered several years in an ascending grade of courts, and always resulted in decrees sustaining the original verdict; and finally the thing got into the supreme court, and there it stuck for twenty years. But last summer, even the supreme court managed to arrive at a decision at last. Once more the original verdict was sustained. Christian then said he was satisfied; but Stavely was present, and whispered to him and to his lawyer, suggesting, "as a mere form," that the original law be exhibited, in order to make sure that it still existed. It seemed an odd idea, but an ingenious one. So the demand was made. A messenger was sent to the magistrate's house; he presently returned with the tidings that it had disappeared from among the state archives.

The court now pronounced its late decision void, since it had been made under a law which had no actual existence.

Great excitement ensued, immediately. The news swept abroad over the whole island that the palladium of the public liberties was lost,—may be treasonably destroyed. Within thirty minutes almost the entire nation were in the court-room,—that is to say, the church. The impeachment of the chief magistrate followed, upon Stavely's motion. The accused met his misfortune with the dignity which became his great office. He did not plead, or even argue: he offered the simple defense that he had not meddled with the missing law; that he had kept the state archives in the same candle-box that had been used as their depository from the beginning; and that he was innocent of the removal or destruction of the lost document.

But nothing could save him; he was found guilty of misprision of treason, and degraded from his office, and all his property was confiscated.

The lamest part of the whole shameful matter was the *reason* suggested by his enemies for his destruction of the law, to wit: that he did it to favor Christian, because Christian was his cousin! Whereas Stavely was the only individual in the entire nation who was *not* his cousin. The reader must remember that all of these people are the descendants of half a dozen men; that the first children intermarried together and bore grandchildren to the mutineers; that these grandchildren intermarried; after them, great and great-great-grandchildren intermarried: so that to-day everybody is blood-kin to everybody. Moreover, the relationships are wonderfully, even astoundingly, mixed up and complicated. A stranger, for instance, says to an islander,—

"You speak of that young woman as your cousin; a while ago you called her your aunt."

"Well, she *is* my aunt, and my cousin too. And also my stepsister, my niece, my fourth cousin, my thirty-third cousin, my forty-second cousin, my great-aunt, my grandmother, my widowed sister-in-law,—and next week she will be my wife."

So the charge of nepotism against the chief magistrate was weak. But no matter; weak or strong, it suited Stavely. Stavely was immediately elected to the vacant magistracy; and, oozing reform from every pore, he went vigorously to work. In no long time religious services raged everywhere and unceasingly. By command, the second prayer of the Sunday morning service, which had customarily endured some thirty-five or forty minutes, and had pleaded for the world, first by continent and then by national and tribal detail, was extended to an hour and a half, and made to include supplications in behalf of the possible peoples in the several planets. Everybody was pleased with this; everybody said, "Now *this* is something *like.*" By command, the usual three-hour sermons were doubled in length. The nation came in a body to testify their gratitude to the new magistrate. The old law forbidding cooking on the Sabbath was extended to the prohibition of eating, also. By command, Sunday-school was privileged to spread over into the week. The joy of all classes was complete. In one short month the new magistrate was become the people's idol!

The time was ripe for this man's next move. He began, cautiously at first, to poison the public mind against England. He took the chief citizens aside, one by one, and conversed with them on this topic. Presently he grew bolder, and spoke out. He said the nation owed it to itself, to its honor, to its great traditions, to rise in its might and throw off "this galling English yoke."

But the simple islanders answered,—

"We had not noticed that it galled. How does it gall? England sends a ship once in three or four years to give us soap and clothing, and things which we sorely need and gratefully receive; but she never troubles us; she lets us go our own way."

"She lets you go your own way! So slaves have felt and spoken in all the ages! This speech shows how fallen you are, how base, how brutalized, you have become, under this grinding tyranny! What! has all manly pride forsaken you? Is liberty nothing? Are you content to be a mere appendage to a foreign and hateful sovereignty, when you might rise up and take your rightful place in the august family of nations, great, free, enlightened, independent, the minion of no sceptred master, but the arbiter of your own destiny, and a voice and a power in decreeing the destinies of your sister-sovereignties of the world?"

Speeches like this produced an effect by and by. Citizens began to feel the English yoke; they did not know exactly how or whereabouts they felt it, but they were perfectly certain they did feel it. They got to grumbling a good deal, and chafing under their chains, and longing for relief and release. They presently fell to hating the English flag, that sign and symbol of their nation's degradation; they ceased to glance up at it as they passed the capitol, but averted their eyes and grated their teeth; and one morning, when it was found trampled into the mud at the foot of the staff, they left it there, and no man put his hand to it to hoist it again. A certain thing which was sure to happen sooner or later happened now. Some of the chief citizens went to the magistrate by night, and said,—

"We can endure this hated tryranny no longer. How can we cast it off?"

By a *coup d'etat.*"

"How?"

"A *coup d'etat.* It is like this: Everything is got ready, and at the appointed moment I, as the official head of the nation, publicly and solemnly proclaim its independence, and absolve it from allegiances to any and all other powers whatsoever."

"That sounds simple and easy. We can do that right away. Then what will be the next thing to do?"

"Seize all the defenses and public properties of all kinds, establish martial law, put the army and navy on a war footing, and proclaim the empire!"

This fine programme dazzled these innocents. They said,—

"This is grand,—this is splendid; but will not England resist?"

"Let her. This rock is a Gibraltar."

"True. But about the empire? Do we *need* an empire, and an emperor?"

"What you *need*, my friends, is unification. Look at Germany; look at Italy. They are unified. Unifications is the thing. It makes living dear. That constitutes progress. We must have a standing army, and a navy. Taxes follow, as a matter of course. All these things summed up make grandeur. With unification and grandeur, what more can you want? Very well,— only the empire can confer these boons."

So on the 8th day of December Pitcairn's Island was proclaimed a free and independent nation; and on the same day the solemn coronation of Butterworth I., emperor of Pitcairn's Island, took place, amid great rejoicings and festivities. The entire nation, with the exception of fourteen persons, mainly little children, marched past the throne in single file, with banners and music, the procession being upwards of ninety feet long; and some said it was as much as three quarters of a minute passing a given point. Nothing like it had ever been seen in the history of the island before. Public enthusiasm was measureless.

Now straightway imperial reforms began. Orders of nobility were instituted. A minister of the navy was appointed, and the whale-boat put in commission. A minister of war was created, and ordered to proceed at once with the formation of a standing army. A first lord of the treasury was named, and commanded to get up a taxation scheme, and also open negotiations for treaties, offensive, defensive, and commercial, with foreign powers. Some generals and admirals were appointed; also some chamberlains, some equerries in waiting, and some lords of the bed-chamber.

At this point all the material was used up. The Grand Duke of Galilee, minister of war, complained that all the sixteen grown men in the empire had been given great offices, and consequently would not consent to serve in the ranks; wherefore his standing army was at a stand-still. The Marquis of Ararat, minister of the navy, made a similar complaint. He said he was willing to steer the whale-boat himself, but he *must* have somebody to man her.

The emperor did the best he could in the circumstances: he took all the boys above the age of ten years away from their mothers, and pressed them into the army, thus constructing a corps of seventeen privates, officered by one lieutenant-general and two major-generals. This pleased the minister of war, but procured the enmity of all the mothers in the land; for they said their precious ones must now find bloody graves in the fields of war, and he would be answerable for it. Some of the more heartbroken and inappeasable among them lay constantly in wait for the emperor and threw yams at him, unmindful of the bodyguard.

On account of the extreme scarcity of material, it was found necessary to require the Duke of Bethany, postmaster-general, to pull stroke-oar in the navy, and thus sit in the rear of a noble of lower degree, namely, Viscount Canaan, lord-justice of the common pleas. This turned the Duke of Bethany into a tolerably open malcontent and a secret conspirator,—a thing which the emperor foresaw, but could not help.

Things went from bad to worse. The emperor raised Nancy Peters to the peerage on one day, and married her the next, notwithstanding, for reasons of state, the cabinet had strenuously advised him to marry Emmeline, eldest daughter of the Archbishop of Bethlehem. This caused trouble in a powerful quarter,—the church. The new empress secured the support and friendship of two thirds of the thirty-six grown women in the nation by absorbing them into her court as maids of honor; but this made deadly enemies of the remaining twelve. The families of the maids of honor soon began to rebel, because there was now nobody at home to keep house. The twelve snubbed women refused to enter the imperial kitchen as servants; so the empress had to require the Countess of Jericho and other great court dames to fetch water, sweep the palace, and perform other menial and equally distasteful services. This made bad blood in that department.

Everybody fell to complaining that the taxes levied for the support of the army, the navy, and the rest of the imperial establishment were intolerably burdensome, and were reducing the nation to beggary. The emperor's reply—"Look at Germany; look at Italy. Are you better than they? and haven't you unification?"—did not satisfy them. They said, "People can't *eat* unification, and we are starving. Agriculture has ceased. Everybody is in the army, everybody is in the navy, everybody is in the public service, standing around in a uniform, with nothing whatever to do, nothing to eat, and nobody to till the fields"—

"Look at Germany; look at Italy. It is the same there. Such is unification, and there's no other way to get it,—no other way to keep it after you've got it," said the poor emperor always.

But the grumblers only replied, "We can't *stand* the taxes,—we can't *stand* them."

Now right on top of this the cabinet reported a national debt amounting to upwards of forty-five dollars,—half a dollar to every individual in the nation. And they proposed to fund something. They had heard that this was always done in such emergencies. They proposed duties on exports; also on imports. And they wanted to issue bonds; also paper money, redeemable in yams and cabbages in fifty years. They said the pay of the army and of the navy and of the whole governmental machine was far in arrears, and unless something was done, and done immediately, national bankruptcy must ensue, and possibly insurrection and revolution. The emperor at once resolved upon a high-handed measure, and one of a nature never before heard of in Pitcairn's Island. He went in state to the church on Sunday morning, with the army at his back, and commanded the minister of the treasury to take up a collection.

That was the feather that broke the camel's back. First one citizen, and then another, rose and refused to submit to this unheard-of outrage,—and each refusal was followed by the immediate confiscation of the malcontent's property. This vigor soon stopped the refusals, and the collection proceeded amid a sullen and ominous silence. As the emperor withdrew with the troops, he said, "I will teach you who is master here." Several persons shouted, "Down with unification!" They were at once arrested and torn from the arms of their weeping friends by the soldiery.

But in the mean time, as any prophet might have foreseen, a Social Democrat had been developed. As the emperor stepped into the gilded imperial wheel-barrow at the church door, the social democrat stabbed at him fifteen or sixteen times with a harpoon, but fortunately with such a peculiarly social democratic unprecision of aim as to do no damage.

That very night the convulsion came. The nation rose as one man,—though forty-nine of the revolutionists were of the other sex. The infantry threw down their pitchforks; the artillery cast aside their cocoa-nuts; the navy revolted; the emperor was seized, and bound hand and foot in his palace. He was very much depressed. He said,—

"I freed you from a grinding tyranny; I lifted you up out of your degradation, and made you a nation among nations; I gave you a strong, compact, centralized government; and, more than all, I gave you the blessing of blessings,—unification. I have done all this, and my reward is hatred, insult, and these bonds. Take me; do with me as ye will. I here resign my crown and all my dignities, and gladly do I release myself from their too heavy burden. For your sake, I took them up; for your sake I lay them down. The imperial jewel is no more; now bruise and defile as ye will the useless setting."

By a unanimous voice the people condemned the ex-emperor and the social democrat to perpetual banishment from church services, or to perpetual labor as galley-slaves in the whale-boat,—whichever they might prefer. The next day the nation assembled again, and rehoisted the British flag, reinstated the British tyranny, reduced the nobility to the condition of commoners again, and then straightway turned their diligent attention to the weeding of the ruined and neglected yam patches, and the rehabilitation of the old useful industries and the old healing and solacing pieties. The ex-emperor restored the lost trespass law, and explained that he had stolen it,—not to injure any one, but to further his political projects. Therefore the nation gave the late chief magistrate his office again, and also his alienated property.

Upon reflection, the ex-emperor and the social democrat chose perpetual banishment from religious services, in preference to perpetual labor as galley-slaves "*with* perpetual religious services," as they phrased it; wherefore the people believed that the poor fellows' troubles had unseated their reason, and so they judged it best to confine them for the present. Which they did.

Such in the history of Pitcairn's "doubtful acquisition."

Goldsmith's Friend Abroad Again
(1870)

Note.—No experience is set down in the following letters which had to be invented. Fancy is not needed to give variety to the history of a Chinaman's sojourn in America. Plain fact is amply sufficient. (*M.T.*)

Letter I

Shanghai, 18—

Dear Ching-Foo:

It is all settled, and I am to leave my oppressed and overburdened native land and cross the sea to that noble realm where all are free and all equal, and none reviled or abused—America! America, whose precious privilege it is to call herself the Land of the Free and the Home of the Brave. We and all that are about us here look over the waves longingly, contrasting the privations of this our birthplace with the opulent comfort of that happy refuge. We know how America has welcomed the Germans and the Frenchmen and the stricken and sorrowing Irish, and we know how she has given them bread and work and liberty, and how grateful they are. And we know that America stands ready to welcome all other oppressed peoples and offer her abundance to all that come, without asking what their nationality is, or their creed or color. And, without being told it, we know that the foreign sufferers she has rescued from oppression and starvation are the most eager of her children to welcome us, because, having suffered themselves, they know what suffering is, and having been generously succored, they long to be generous to other unfortunates and thus show that magnanimity is not wasted upon them.

AH SONG HI

LETTER II

At Sea, 18—

DEAR CHING-FOO:

We are far away at sea now, on our way to the beautiful Land of the Free and Home of the Brave. We shall soon be where all men are alike, and where sorrow is not known.

The good American who hired me to go to his country is to pay me $12 a month, which is immense wages, you know—twenty times as much as one gets in China. My passage in the ship is a very large sum—indeed, it is a fortune—and this I must pay myself eventually, but I am allowed ample time to make it good to my employer in, he advancing it now. For a mere form, I have turned over my wife, my boy, and my two daughters to my employer's partner for security for the payment of the ship fare. But my employer says they are in no danger of being sold, for he knows I will be faithful to him, and that is the main security.

I thought I would have twelve dollars to begin life with in America, but the American Consul took two of them for making a certificate that I was shipped on the steamer. He has no right to do more than charge the ship two dollars for *one* certificate for the *ship,* with the number of her Chinese passengers set down in it; but he chooses to force a certificate upon each and every Chinaman and put the two dollars in his pocket. As 1,300 of my countrymen are in this vessel, the Consul received $2,600 for certificates. My employer tells me that the Government at Washington know of this fraud, and are so bitterly opposed to the existence of such a wrong that they tried hard to have the extor—— the fee, I mean, legalized by the last Congress; but as the bill did not pass, the Consul will have to take the fee dishonestly until next Congress makes it legitimate. It is a great and good and noble country, and hates all forms of vice and chicanery.

We are in that part of the vessel always reserved for my countrymen. It is called the steerage. It is kept for us, my employer says, because it is not subject to changes of temperature and dangerous drafts of air. It is only another instance of the loving unselfishness of the Americans for all unfortunate foreigners. The steerage is a little crowded, and rather warm and close, but no doubt it is best for us that it should be so.

Yesterday our people got to quarrelling among themselves, and the captain turned a volume of hot steam upon a mass of them and scalded eighty or ninety of them more or less severely. Flakes and ribbons of skin came off some of them. There was wild shrieking and struggling while the vapor enveloped the great throng, and so some who were not scalded got trampled upon and hurt. We do not complain, for my employer says this is the usual way of quieting disturbances on board the ship, and that it is done in the cabins among the Americans every day or two.

Congratulate me, Ching-Foo! In ten days more I shall step upon the shore of America, and be received by her great-hearted people; and I shall straighten myself up and feel that I am a free man among freemen.

AH SONG HI

LETTER III

San Francisco, 18—

DEAR CHING-FOO:

I stepped ashore jubilant! I wanted to dance, shout, sing, worship the generous Land of the Free and Home of the Brave. But as I walked from the gangplank a man in a gray uniform kicked me violently behind and told me to look out—so my employer translated it. As I turned, another officer of the same kind struck me with a short club and also instructed me to look out. I was about to take hold of my end of the pole which had mine and Hong-Wo's basket and things suspended from it, when a third officer hit me with his club to signify that I was to drop it, and then kicked me to signify that he was satisfied with my promptness. Another person came now, and searched all through our basket and bundles, emptying everything out on the dirty wharf. Then this person and another searched us all over. They found a little package of opium sewed into the artificial part of Hong-Wo's queue, and they took that, and also they made him prisoner and handed him over to an officer, who marched him away. They took his luggage, too, because of his crime, and as our luggage was so mixed together that they could not tell mine from his, they took it all. When I offered to help divide it, they kicked me and desired me to look out.

Having now no baggage and no companion, I told my employer that if he was willing, I would walk about a little and see the city and people until he needed me. I did not like to seem disappointed with my reception in the good land of refuge for the oppressed, and so I looked and spoke as cheerily as I could. But he said, wait a minute—I must be vaccinated to prevent my taking the small-pox. I smiled and said I had already had the small-pox, as he could see by the marks, and so I need not wait to be "vaccinated," as he called it. But he said it was the law, and I must be vaccinated anyhow. The doctor would never let me pass, for the law obliged him to vaccinate all Chinamen and charge them *ten dollars apiece* for it, and I might be sure that no doctor who would be the servant of that law would let a fee slip through his fingers to accommodate any absurd fool who had seen fit to have the disease in some other country. And presently the doctor came and did his work and took my last penny—my ten dollars which were the hard savings of nearly a year and a half of labor and privation. Ah, if the law-makers had only known there were plenty of doctors in the city glad of a chance to vaccinate people for a dollar or two, they would never have put the price up so high against a poor friendless Irish, or Italian, or Chinese pauper fleeing to the good land to escape hunger and hard times.

AH SONG HI

LETTER IV

San Francisco, 18—

DEAR CHING-FOO:

I have been here about a month now, and am learning a little of the language every day. My employer was disappointed in the matter of hiring us out to service on the plantations in the far eastern portion of this continent. His enterprise was a failure, and so he set us all free, merely taking measures to secure to himself the repayment of the passage money which he paid for us. We are to make this good to him out of the first moneys we earn here. He says it is sixty dollars apiece.

We were thus set free about two weeks after we reached here. We had been massed together in some small houses up to that time, waiting. I walked forth to seek my fortune. I was to begin life a stranger in a strange land, without a friend, or a penny, or any clothes but those I had on my back. I had not any advantage on my side in the world—not one, except good health and the lack of any necessity to waste any time or anxiety on the watching of my baggage. No, I forget. I reflected that I had one prodigious advantage over paupers in other lands—I was in America! I was in the heaven-provided refuge of the oppressed and the forsaken!

Just as that comforting thought passed through my mind, some young men set a fierce dog on me. I tried to defend myself, but could do nothing. I retreated to the recess of a closed doorway, and there the dog had me at his mercy, flying at my throat and face or any part of my body that presented itself. I shrieked for help, but the young men only jeered and laughed. Two men in gray uniforms (policemen is their official title) looked on for a minute and then walked leisurely away. But a man stopped them and brought them back and told them it was a shame to leave me in such distress. Then the two policemen beat off the dog with small clubs, and a comfort it was to be rid of him, though I was just rags and blood from head to foot. The man who brought the policemen asked the young men why they abused me in that way, and they said they didn't want any of his meddling. And they said to him:

"This Ching divil comes till Ameriky to take the bread out o' dacent intilligent white men's mouths, and whin they try to defind their rights there's a dale o' fuss made about it."

They began to threaten my benefactor, and as he saw no friendliness in the faces that had gathered meanwhile, he went on his way. He got many a curse when he was gone. The policemen now told me I was under arrest and must go with them. I asked one of them what wrong I had done to any one that I should be arrested, and he only struck me with his club and ordered me to "hold my yop." With a jeering crowd of street boys and loafers at my heels, I was taken up an alley and into a stone-paved dungeon which had large cells all down one side of it, with iron gates to them. I stood up by a desk while a man behind it wrote down certain things about me on a slate. One of my captors said:

"Enter a charge against this Chinaman of being disorderly and disturbing the peace."

I attempted to say a word, but he said:

"Silence! Now ye had better go slow, my good fellow. This is two or three times you've tried to get off some of your d—d insolence. Lip won't do here. You've *got* to simmer down, and if you don't take to it paceable we'll see if we can't make you. Fat's your name?"

"Ah Song Hi."

"Alias what?"

I said I did not understand, and he said what he wanted was my *true* name, for he guessed I picked up this one since I stole my last chickens. They all laughed loudly at that.

Then they searched me. They found nothing, of course. They seemed very angry and asked who I supposed would "go my bail or pay my fine." When they explained these things to me, I said I had done nobody any harm, and why should I need to have bail or pay a fine? Both of them kicked me and warned me that I would find it to my advantage to try and be as civil as convenient. I protested that I had not meant anything disrespectful. Then one of them took me to one side and said:

"Now look here, Johnny, it's no use you playing softy wid us. We mane business, ye know; and the sooner ye put us on the scent of a V, the asier ye'll save yerself from a dale of trouble. Ye can't get out o' this for anny less. Who's your frinds?"

I told him I had not a single friend in all the land of America, and that I was far from home and help, and very poor. And I begged him to let me go.

He gathered the slack of my blouse collar in his grip and jerked and shoved and hauled at me across the dungeon, and then unlocking an iron cell-gate thrust me in with a kick and said:

"Rot there, ye furrin spawn, till ye lairn that there's no room in America for the likes of ye or your nation."

AH SONG HI

LETTER V

San Francisco, 18—

DEAR CHING-FOO:

You will remember that I had just been thrust violently into a cell in the city prison when I wrote last. I stumbled and fell on some one. I got a blow and a curse; and on top of these a kick or two and a shove. In a second or two it was plain that I was in a nest of prisoners and was being "passed around"—for the instant I was knocked out of the way of one I fell on the head or heels of another and was promptly ejected, only to land on a third prisoner and get a new contribution of kicks and curses and a new destination. I brought up at last in an unoccupied corner, very much battered and bruised and sore, but glad enough to be let alone for a little while. I was on the flag-stones, for there was no furniture in the den except a long, broad board, or a combination of boards, like a barn door, and this bed was accommodating five or six persons, and that was its full capacity.

They lay stretched side by side, snoring—when not fighting. One end of the board was four inches higher than the other, and so the slant answered for a pillow. There were no blankets, and the night was a little chilly; the nights are always a little chilly in San Francisco, though never severely cold. The board was a deal more comfortable than the stones, and occasionally some flag-stone plebeian like me would try to creep to a place on it; and then the aristocrats would hammer him good and make him think a flag pavement was a nice enough place after all.

I lay quiet in my corner, stroking my bruises and listening to the revelations the prisoners made to each other—and to me—for some that were near me talked to me a good deal. I had long had an idea that Americans, being free, had no need of prisons, which are a contrivance of despots for keeping restless patriots out of mischief. So I was considerably surprised to find out my mistake.

Ours was a big general cell, it seemed, for the temporary accommodation of all comers whose crimes were trifling. Among us there were two Americans, two "Greasers" (Mexicans), a Frenchman, a German, four Irishmen, a Chilenean (and, in the next cell, only separated from us by a grating, two women), all drunk, and all more or less noisy; and as night fell and advanced, they grew more and more discontented and disorderly, occasionally shaking the prison bars and glaring through them at the slowly pacing officer, and cursing him with all their hearts. The two women were nearly middle-aged, and they had only had enough liquor to stimulate instead of stupefy them. Consequently they would fondle and kiss each other for some minutes, and then fall to fighting and keep it up till they were just two grotesque tangles of rags and blood and tumbled hair. Then they would rest awhile, and pant and swear. While they were affectionate they always spoke of each other as "ladies," but while they were fighting "strumpet" was the mildest name they could think of—and they could only make that do by tacking some sounding profanity to it. In their last fight, which was toward midnight, one of them bit off the other's finger, and then the officer interfered and put the "Greaser" into the "dark cell" to answer for it—because the woman that did it laid it on him, and the other woman did not deny it because, as she said afterward, she "wanted another crack at the huzzy when her finger quit hurting," and so she did not want her removed. By this time those two women had mutilated each other's clothes to that extent that there was not sufficient left to cover their nakedness. I found that one of these creatures had spent nine years in the county jail, and that the other one had spent about four or five years in the same place. They had done it from choice. As soon as they were discharged from captivity they would go straight and get drunk, and then steal some trifling thing while an officer was observing them. That would entitle them to another two months in jail, and there they would occupy clean, airy apartments, and have good food in plenty, and being at no expense at all, they could make shirts for the clothiers at half a dollar apiece and thus keep themselves in smoking tobacco and such other luxuries as they wanted. When the two months were up, they would go just as straight as they could walk to Mother Leonard's and get drunk; and from there to Kearny street and steal something; and thence to this city prison, and next day back to the old quarters in the county jail again. One of them had really kept this up for nine years and the other four or five, and both said they meant to end their days in that prison. Finally, both these creatures fell upon me while I was dozing with my head against their grating, and battered me considerably, because they discovered that I was a Chinaman, and they said I was "a bloody interlopin' loafer come from the divil's own country to take the bread out of dacent people's mouths and put down the wages for work whin it was all a Christian could do to kape body and sowl together as it was." "Loafer" means one who will not work.

AH SONG HI

LETTER VI

San Francisco, 18—

DEAR CHING-FOO:

To continue—the two women became reconciled to each other again through the common bond of interest and sympathy created between them by pounding me in partnership, and when they had finished me they fell to embracing each other again and swearing more eternal affection like that which had subsisted between them all the evening, barring occasional interruptions. They agreed to swear the finger-biting on the Greaser in open court, and get him sent to the penitentiary for the crime of mayhem.

Another of our company was a boy of fourteen who had been watched for some time by officers and teachers, and repeatedly detected in enticing young girls from the public schools to the lodgings of gentlemen down town. He had been furnished with lures in the form of pictures and books of a peculiar kind, and these he had distributed among his clients. There were likenesses of fifteen of these young girls on exhibition (only to prominent citizens and persons in authority, it was said, though most people came to get a sight) at the police headquarters, but no punishment at all was to be inflicted on the poor little misses. The boy was afterward sent into captivity at the House of Correction for some months, and there was a strong disposition to punish the gentlemen who had employed the boy to entice the girls, but as that could not be done without making public the names of those gentlemen and thus injuring them socially, the idea was finally given up.

There was also in our cell that night a photographer (a kind of artist who makes likenesses of people with a machine), who had been for some time patching the pictured heads of well-known and respectable young ladies to the nude, pictured bodies of another class women; then from this patched creation he would make photographs and sell them privately at high prices to rowdies and blackguards, averring that these, the best young ladies of the city, had hired him to take their likenesses in that unclad condition. What a lecture the police judge read that photographer when he was convicted! He told him his crime was little less than an outrage. He abused that photographer till he almost made him sink through the floor, and then he fined him a hundred dollars. And he told him he might consider himself lucky that he didn't fine him a hundred and twenty-five dollars. They are awfully severe on crime here.

About two or two and a half hours after midnight, of that first experience of mine in the city prison, such of us as were dozing were awakened by a noise of beating and dragging and groaning, and in a little while a man was pushed into our den with a "There, d—n you, soak there a spell!"—and then the gate was closed and the officers went away again. The man who was thrust among us fell limp and helpless by the grating, but as nobody could reach him with a kick without the trouble of hitching along toward him or getting fairly up to deliver it, our people only grumbled at him, and cursed him, and called him insulting names—for misery and hardship do not make their victims gentle or charitable toward each other. But as he neither tried humbly to conciliate our people nor swore back at them, his unnatural conduct created surprise, and several of the party crawled to him where he lay in the dim light that came through the grating, and examined into his case. His head was very bloody and his wits were gone. After about an hour, he sat up and stared around; then his eyes grew more natural and he began to tell how that he was going along with a bag on his shoulder and a brace of policemen ordered him to stop, which he did not do—was chased and caught, beaten ferociously about the head on the way to the prison and after arrival there, and finally thrown into our den like a dog. And in a few seconds he sank down again and grew flighty of speech. One of our people was at last penetrated with something vaguely akin to compassion, may be, for he looked out through the gratings at the guardian officer pacing to and fro, and said:

"Say, Mickey, this shrimp's goin' to die."

"Stop your noise!" was all the answer he got. But presently our man tried it again. He drew himself to the gratings, grasping them with his hands, and looking out through them, sat waiting till the officer was passing once more, and then said:

"Sweetness, you'd better mind your eye, now, because you beats have killed this cuss. You've busted his head and he'll pass in his checks before sun-up. You better go for a doctor, now, you bet you had."

The officer delivered a sudden rap on our man's knuckles with his club, that sent him scampering and howling among the sleeping forms on the flag-stones, and an answering burst of laughter came from the half dozen policemen idling about the railed desk in the middle of the dungeon.

But there was a putting of heads together out there presently, and a conversing in low voices, which seemed to show that our man's talk had made an impression; and presently an officer went away in a hurry, and shortly came back with a person who entered our cell and felt the bruised man's pulse and threw the glare of a lantern on his drawn face, striped with blood, and his glassy eyes, fixed and vacant. The doctor examined the man's broken head also, and presently said:

"If you'd called me an hour ago I might have saved this man, may be—too late now."

Then he walked out into the dungeon and the officers surrounded him, and they kept up a low and earnest buzzing of conversation for fifteen minutes, I should think, and then the doctor took his departure from the prison. Several of the officers now came in and worked a little with the wounded man, but toward daylight he died.

It was the longest, longest night! And when the daylight came filtering reluctantly into the dungeon at last, it was the grayest, dreariest, saddest daylight! And yet, when an officer by and by turned off the sickly yellow gas flame, and immediately the gray of dawn became fresh and white, there was a lifting of my spirits that acknowledged and believed that the night *was* gone, and straightway I fell to stretching my sore limbs, and looking about me with a grateful sense of relief and a returning interest in life. About me lay the evidences that what seemed now a feverish dream and a nightmare was the memory of a reality instead. For on the boards lay four frowsy, ragged, bearded vagabonds, snoring—one turned end-for-end and resting an unclean foot, in a ruined stocking, on the hairy breast of a neighbor; the young boy was uneasy, and lay moaning in his sleep; other forms lay half revealed and half concealed about the floor; in the furthest corner the gray light fell upon a sheet, whose elevations and depressions indicated the places of the dead man's face and feet and folded hands; and through the dividing bars one could discern the almost nude forms of the two exiles from the county jail twined together in a drunken embrace, and sodden with sleep.

By and by all the animals in all the cages awoke,

and stretched themselves, and exchanged a few cuffs and curses, and then began to clamor for breakfast. Breakfast was brought in at last—bread and beef-steak on tin plates, and black coffee in tin cups, and no grabbing allowed. And after several dreary hours of waiting, after this, we were all marched out into the dungeon and joined there by all manner of vagrants and vagabonds, of all shades and colors and nationalities, from the other cells and cages of the place; and pretty soon our whole menagerie was marched up stairs and locked fast behind a high railing in a dirty room with a dirty audience in it. And this audience stared at us, and at a man seated on high behind what they call a pulpit in this country, and at some clerks and other officials seated below him—and waited. This was the police court.

The court opened. Pretty soon I was compelled to notice that a culprit's nationality made for or against him in this court. Overwhelming proofs were necessary to convict an Irishman of crime, and even then his punishment amounted to little; Frenchmen, Spaniards, and Italians had strict and unprejudiced justice meted out to them, in exact accordance with the evidence; negroes were promptly punished, when there was the slightest preponderance of testimony against them; but Chinamen were punished *always*, apparently. Now this gave me some uneasiness, I confess. I knew that this state of things must of necessity be accidental, because in this country all men were free and equal, and one person could not take to himself an advantage not accorded to all other individuals. I knew that, and yet in spite of it I was uneasy.

And I grew still more uneasy, when I found that any succored and befriended refugee from Ireland or elsewhere could stand up before that judge and swear away the life or liberty or character of a refugee from China; but that by the law of the land *the Chinaman could not testify against the Irishman.* I was really and truly uneasy, but still my faith in the universal liberty that America accords and defends, and my deep veneration for the land that offered all distressed outcasts a home and protection, was strong within me, and I said to myself that it would all come out right yet.

AH SONG HI

LETTER VII

San Francisco, 18—

DEAR CHING-FOO:

I was glad enough when my case came up. An hour's experience had made me as tired of the police court as of the dungeon. I was not uneasy about the result of the trial, but on the contrary felt that as soon as the large auditory of Americans present should hear how that the rowdies had set the dogs on me when I was going peacefully along the street, and how, when I was all torn and bleeding, the officers arrested *me* and put me in jail and let the rowdies go free, the gallant hatred of oppression which is part of the very flesh and blood of every American would be stirred to its utmost, and I should be instantly set at liberty. In truth I began to fear for the other side. There in full view stood the ruffians who had misused me, and I began to fear that in the first burst of generous anger occasioned by the revealment of what they had done, they might be harshly handled, and possibly even banished the country as having dishonored her and being no longer worthy to remain upon her sacred soil.

The official interpreter of the court asked my name, and then spoke it aloud so that all could hear. Supposing that all was now ready, I cleared my throat and began—in Chinese, because of my imperfect English:

"Hear, O high and mighty mandarin, and believe! As I went about my peaceful business in the street, behold certain men set a dog on me, and—"

"Silence!"—

It was the judge that spoke. The interpreter whispered to me that I must keep perfectly still. He said that no statement would be received from me—I must only talk through my lawyer.

I had no lawyer. In the early morning a police court lawyer (termed, in the higher circles of society, a "shyster") had come into our den in the prison and offered his services to me, but I had been obliged to go without them because I could not pay in advance or give security. I told the interpreter how the matter stood. He said I must take my chances on the witnesses then. I glanced around, and my failing confidence revived.

"Call those four Chinamen yonder," I said. "They saw it all. I remember their faces perfectly. They will prove that the white men set the dog on me when I was not harming them."

"That won't work," said he. "In this country white men can testify against Chinamen all they want to, but *Chinamen ain't allowed to testify against white men!"*

What a chill went through me! And then I felt the indignant blood rise to my cheek at this libel upon the Home of the Oppressed, where all men are free and equal—perfectly equal—perfectly free and perfectly equal. I despised this Chinese-speaking Spaniard for his mean slander of the land that was sheltering and feeding him. I sorely wanted to sear his eyes with that sentence from the great and good American Declaration of Independence which we have copied in letters of gold in China and keep hung up over our family altars and in our temples—I mean the one about all men being created free and equal.

But woe is me, Ching-Foo, the man was right. He was right, after all. There were my witnesses, but I could not use them. But now came a new hope. I saw my white friend come in, and I felt that he had come there purposely to help me. I may almost say I knew it. So I grew easier. He passed near enough to me to say under his breath, "Don't be afraid," and then I had no more fear. But presently the rowdies recognized him and began to scowl at him in no friendly way, and to make threatening signs at him. The two officers that arrested me fixed their eyes steadily on his; he bore it well, but gave in presently, and dropped his eyes. They still gazed at his eyebrows, and every time he raised his eyes he encountered their winkless stare—until after a minute or two he ceased to lift his head at all. The judge had been giving some instructions privately to some one for a little while, but now he was ready to resume business. Then the trial so unspeakably important to me, and freighted with such prodigious consequence to my wife and children, began, progressed, ended, was recorded in the books, noted down by the newspaper reporters, and *forgotten* by everybody but me—all in the little space of two minutes!

"Ah Song Hi, Chinaman. Officers O'Flannigan and O'Flaherty, witnesses. Come forward, Officer O'Flannigan."

OFFICER—"He was making a disturbance in Kearny street."

JUDGE—"Any witnesses on the other side?"

No response. The white friend raised his eyes—encountered Officer O'Flaherty's—blushed a little—got up and left the courtroom, avoiding all glances and not taking his own from the floor.

JUDGE—"Give him five dollars or ten days."

In my desolation there was a glad surprise in the words; but it passed away when I found that he only meant that I was to be fined five dollars or imprisoned ten days longer in default of it.

There were twelve or fifteen Chinamen in our crowd of prisoners, charged with all manner of little thefts and misdemeanors, and their cases were quickly disposed of, as a general thing. When the charge came from a policeman or other white man, he made his statement and that was the end of it, unless the Chinaman's lawyer could find some white person to testify in his client's behalf; for, neither the accused Chinaman nor his countrymen being allowed to say anything, the statement of the officers or other white person was amply sufficient to convict. So, as I said, the Chinamen's cases were quickly disposed of, and fines and imprisonment promptly distributed among them. In one or two of the cases the charges against Chinamen were brought by Chinamen themselves, and in those cases Chinamen testified against Chinamen, through the interpreter; but the fixed rule of the court being that the *preponderance* of testimony in such cases should determine the prisoner's guilt or innocence, and there being nothing very binding about an oath administered to the lower orders of our people without the ancient solemnity of cutting off a chicken's head and burning some yellow paper at the same time, the interested parties naturally drum up a cloud of witnesses who are cheerfully willing to give evidence without ever knowing anything about the matter in hand. The judge has a custom of rattling through with as much of this testimony as his patience will stand, and then shutting off the rest and striking an average.

By noon all the business of the court was finished, and then several of us who had not fared well were remanded to prison; the judge went home; the lawyers, and officers, and spectators departed their several ways, and left the uncomely court-room to silence, solitude, and Stiggers, the newspaper reporter, which latter would now write up his items (said an ancient Chinaman to me), in the which he would praise all the policemen indiscriminately and abuse the Chinamen and dead people.

Ah Song Hi

A True Story, Repeated Word for Word as I Heard It (1874)

It was summer time, and twilight. We were sitting on the porch of the farm-house, on the summit of the hill, and "Aunt Rachel" was sitting respectfully below our level, on the steps,—for she was our servant, and colored. She was of mighty frame and stature; she was sixty years old, but her eye was undimmed and her strength unabated. She was a cheerful, hearty soul, and it was no more trouble for her to laugh than it is for a bird to sing. She was under fire, now, as usual when the day was done. That is to say, she was being chaffed without mercy, and was enjoying it. She would let off peal after peal of laughter, and then sit with her face in her hands and shake with throes of enjoyment which she could no longer get breath enough to express. At such a moment as this a thought occurred to me, and I said:

"Aunt Rachel, how is it that you've lived sixty years and never had any trouble?"

She stopped quaking. She paused, and there was a moment of silence. She turned her face over her shoulder toward me, and said, without even a smile in her voice:—

"Misto C——, is you in 'arnest?"

It surprised me a good deal; and it sobered my manner and my speech, too. I said:—

"Why, I thought—that is, I meant—why, you *can't* have had any trouble. I've never heard you sigh, and never seen your eye when there wasn't a laugh in it."

She faced fairly around, now, and was full of earnestness.

"Has I had any trouble? Misto C——, I's gwyne to tell you, den I leave it to you. I was bawn down 'mongst de slaves; I knows all 'bout slavery, 'case I ben one of 'em my own se'f. Well, sah, my ole man —dat's my husban'—he was lovin' an' kind to me, jist as kind as you is to yo' own wife. An' we had chil'en—seven chil'en. Dey was black, but de Lord can't make no chil'en so black but what dey mother loves 'em an' wouldn't give 'em up, no, not for anything dat's in dis whole world.

"Well sah, I was raised in ole Fo'ginny, but my mother she was raised in Maryland; an' my *souls!* she was turrible when she'd git started! My *lan'!* but she'd make de fur fly! When she'd git into dem tantrums, she always had one word dat she said. She'd straighten herse'f up an' put her fists in her hips an' say, 'I want you to understan' dat I wa'nt bawn in the mash to be fool' by trash! I's one o' de ole Blue Hen's Chickens, *I* is!' 'Ca'se, you see, dat's what folks dat's bawn in Maryland calls deyselves, an' dey's proud of it. Well, dat was her word. I don't ever forgit it, beca'se she said it so much, an' beca'se she said it one day when my little Henry tore his wris' awful, and most busted his head, right up at de top of his forehead, an' de niggers didn't fly aroun' fas' enough to 'tend to him. An' when dey talk' back at her, she up an' she says, 'Look-a-heah!' she says, 'I want you niggers to understan' dat I wa'nt bawn in de mash to be fool' by trash! I's one o' de ole Blue Hen's Chickens, *I* is!' an' den she clar' dat kitchen an' bandage' up de chile herse'f. So I says dat word, too, when I's riled.

"Well, bymeby my ole mistis say she's broke, an' she's got to sell all the niggers on de place. An' when I heah dat dey gwyne to sell us all off at oction in Richmon', oh de good gracious! I know what dat mean!"

Aunt Rachel had gradually risen, while she warmed to her subject, and now she towered above us, black against the stars.

"Dey put chains on us an' put us on a stan' as high as dis po'ch,—twenty foot high,—an' all de people stood aroun', crowds an' crowds. An' dey'd come up dah an' look at us all roun', an' squeeze our arm, an' make us git up an' walk, an' den say, 'Dis one too ole,' or 'Dis one lame,' or 'Dis one don't 'mount to much.' An' dey sole my ole man, an' took him away, an' dey begin to sell my chil'en an' take *dem* away, an' I begin to cry; an' de man say, 'Shet up yo' dam blubberin',' an' hit me on de mouf wid his han'. An' when de las' one was gone but my little Henry, I grab' *him* clost up to my breas' so, an' I ris up an' says, 'You shan't take him away,' I says; 'I'll kill de man dat tetches him!' I says. But my little Henry whisper an' say, 'I gwyne to run away, an' den I work an' buy you' freedom.' Oh, bless de chile, he always so good! But dey got him—dey got him, de men did; but I took and tear de clo'es mos' off of 'em an' beat 'em over de head wid my chain; an' *dey* give it to *me*, too, but I didn't mine dat.

"Well, dah was my ole man gone, an' all my chil'en, all my seven chil'en—an' six of 'em I hain't set eyes on ag'in to dis day, an' dat's twenty-two year ago las' Easter. De man dat bought me b'long' in Newbern, an' he took me dah. Well, bymeby de years roll on an' de waw come. My marster he was a Confedrit colonel, an' I was his family's cook. So when de Unions took dat town, dey all run away an' lef' me all by myse'f wid de other niggers in dat mons'us big house. So de big Union officers move in dah, an' dey ask me would I cook for *dem.* 'Lord bless you,' says I, 'dat's what I's *for.*'

"Dey wa'nt no small-fry officers, mine you, dey was de biggest dey *is;* an' de way dey made dem sojers mosey roun'! De Gen'l he tole me to boss dat kitchen; an' he say, 'If anybody come meddlin' wid you, you jist make 'em walk chalk; don't you be afeared,' he say; 'you's 'mong frens, now.'

"Well, I thinks to myse'f, if my little Henry ever got a chance to run away, he'd make to de Norf, o' course. So one day I comes in dah whar de big officers was, in de parlor, an' I drops a kurtchy, so, an' I up an' tole 'em 'bout my Henry, dey a-listenin' to my troubles jist de same as if I was white folks; an' I says, 'What I come for is beca'se if he got away and got up Norf whar you gemmen comes from, you might 'a' seen him, maybe, an' could tell me so as I could fine him ag'in; he was very little, an' he had a sk-yar on his lef' wris', an' at de top of his forehead.' Den dey look mournful, an' de Gen'l say, 'How long sence you los' him?' an' I say, 'Thirteen year.' Den de Gen'l say, 'He wouldn't be little no mo', now—he's a man!'

"I never thought o' dat befo'! He was only dat little feller to *me*, yit. I never thought 'bout him growin' up an' bein' big. But I see it den. None o' de gemmen had run acrost him, so dey couldn't do nothin' for me. But all dat time, do' *I* didn't know it, my Henry *was* run off to de Norf, years an' years, an' he was a barber, too, an' worked for hisse'f. An' bymeby, when de waw come' he ups an' he says: 'I's done barberin',' he says, 'I's gwyne to fine my ole mammy, less'n she's dead.' So he sole out an' went to whar dey was recruitin', an' hired hisse'f out to de colonel for his servant; an' den he went all froo de battles everywhah, huntin' for his ole mammy; yes indeedy, he'd heir to fust one officer an' den another, till he'd ransacked de whole Souf; but you see *I* didn't know nuffin 'bout *dis.* How was *I* gwyne to know it?

"Well, one night we had a big sojer ball; de sojers dah at Newbern was always havin' balls an' carryin' on. Dey had 'em in my kitchen, heaps o' times, 'ca'se it was so big. Mine you, I was *down* on sich doin's; beca'se my place was wide de officers, an' it rasp me to have dem common sojers cavortin' roun' my kitchen like dat. But I alway' stood aroun' an' kep' things straight, I did; an' sometimes dey'd git my dander up, an' den I'd make 'em clar dat kitchen, mine I *tell* you!

"Well, one night—it was a Friday night—dey comes a whole plattoon f'm a *nigger* ridgment dat was on guard at de house,—de house was headquarters, you know,—an' den I was jist a-*bilin'!* Mad? I was jist a-*boomin'!* I swelled aroun', an' swelled aroun'; I jist was a-itchin' for 'em to do somefin for to start me. *An'* dey was a-waltzin' an' a-dancin'! *my!* but dey was havin' a time! an' I jist a-swellin' an' a-swellin' up! Pooty soon, 'long comes *sich* a spruce young nigger a-sailin' down de room wid a yaller wench roun' de wais'; an' roun' an' roun' an' roun' dey went, enough to make a body drunk to look at 'em; an' when dey got abreas' o' me, dey went to kin' o' balancin' aroun' fust on one leg an' den on t'other, an' smilin' at my big red turban, an' makin' fun, an' I ups an' says '*Git* along wid you!—rubbage!' De young man's face kin' o' changed, all of a sudden, for 'bout a second, but den he went to smilin' ag'in, same as he was befo'. Well, 'bout dis time, in comes some niggers dat played music and b'lon' to de ban', an' dey *never* could git along widout puttin' on airs. An' de very fust air dey put on dat night, I lit into 'em! Dey laughed, an' dat made me wuss. De res' o' de niggers got to laughin', an' den my soul *alive* but I was hot! My eye was jist a-blazin'! I jist straightened myself up, so,—jist as I is now, plum to de ceilin', mos',—an' I digs my fists into my hips, an' I says, 'Look-a-heah!' I says, 'I want you niggers to understan' dat I wa'nt bawn in de mash to be fool' by trash! I's one o' de ole Blue Hen's Chickens, *I* is!' an' den I see dat young man stan' a-starin' an' stiff, lookin' kin' o' up at de ceilin' like he fo'got somefin, an' couldn't 'member it no mo'. Well, I jist march' on dem niggers,—so, lookin' like a gen'l,—an' dey cave' away befo' me an' out at de do'. An' as dis young man was a-goin' out, I heah him say to another nigger, 'Jim,' he says, 'you go 'long an' tell de cap'n I be on han' 'bout eight o'clock in de mawnin'; dey's somefin on my mine, he says; 'I don't sleep no mo' dis night. You go 'long,' he says, 'an' leave me by my own se'f.'

"Dis was 'bout one o'clock in de mawnin'. Well, 'bout seven, I was up an' on han', gittin' de officers' breakfast. I was a-stoopin' down by de stove,—jist so, same as if yo' foot was de stove,—an' I'd opened de stove do' wid my right han',—so, pushin' it back, jist as I pushes you' foot,—an' I'd jist got de pan o' hot biscuits in my han' an' was 'bout to raise up, when I see a black face come aroun' under mine, an' de eyes a-lookin' up into mine, jist as I's a-lookin' up clost under you' face now; an' I jist stopped *right dah,* an' never budged! jist gazed, an' gazed, so; an' de pan begin to tremble, an' all of a sudden I *knowed!* De pan drop' on de flo' an' I grab his lef' han' an' shove back his sleeve,—jist so, as I's doin' to you,—an' den I goes for his forehead an' push de hair back, so, an' 'Boy!' I says, 'if you an't my Henry, what is you doin' wid dis welt on yo' wris' an' dat sk-yar on you' forehead? De Lord God ob heaven be praise', I got my own ag'in!'

"Oh, no Misto C——, *I* hain't had no trouble. An' no *joy!*"

About Smells
(1870)

In a recent issue of the "Independent," the Rev. T. De Witt Talmage, of Brooklyn, has the following utterance on the subject of "Smells":

I have a good Christian friend who, if he sat in the front pew in church, and a working man should enter the door at the other end, would smell him instantly. My friend is not to blame for the sensitiveness of his nose, any more than you would flog a pointer for being keener on the scent than a stupid watch-dog. The fact is, if you had all the churches free, by reason of the miving up of the common people with the uncommon, you would keep one-half of Christendom sick at their stomach. If you are going to kill the church thus with bad smells, I will have nothing to do with this work of evangelization.

We have reason to believe that there will be laboring men in heaven; and also a number of negroes, and Esquimaux, and Tierra del Fuegans, and Arabs, and a few Indians, and possibly even some Spaniards and Portuguese. All things are possible with God. We shall have all these sorts of people in heaven; but, alas! in getting them we shall lose the society of Dr. Talmage. Which is to say, we shall lose the company of one who could give more real "tone" to celestial society than any other contribution Brooklyn could furnish. And what would eternal happiness be without the Doctor? Blissful, unquestionably—we know that well enough—but would it be *distingué*, would it be *recherché* without him? St. Matthew without stockings or sandals; St. Jerome bareheaded, and with a coarse brown blanket robe dragging the ground; St. Sebastian with scarcely any raiment at all—these we should see, and should enjoy seeing them; but would we not miss a spike-tailed coat and kids, and turn away regretfully, and say to parties from the Orient: "These are well enough, but you ought to see Talmage of Brooklyn." I fear me that in the better world we shall not even have Dr. Talmage's "good Christian friend." For if he were sitting under the glory of the Throne, and the keeper of the keys admitted a Benjamin Franklin or other laboring man, that "friend," with his fine natural powers infinitely augmented by emancipation from hampering flesh, would detect him with a single sniff, and immediately take his hat and ask to be excused.

To all outward seeming, the Rev. T. De Witt Talmage is of the same material as that used in the construction of his early predecessors in the ministry; and yet one feels that there must be a difference somewhere between him and the Saviour's first disciples. It may be because here, in the nineteenth century, Dr. T. has had advantages which Paul and Peter and the others could not and did not have. There was a lack of polish about them, and a looseness of etiquette, and a want of exclusiveness, which one cannot help noticing. They healed the very beggars, and held intercourse with people of a villainous odor every day. If the subject of these remarks had been chosen among the original Twelve Apostles, he would not have associated with the rest, because he could not have stood the fishy smell of some of his comrades who came from around the Sea of Galilee. He would have resigned his commission with some such remark as he makes in the extract quoted above: "Master, if thou art going to kill the church thus with bad smells, I will have nothing to do with this work of evangelization." He is a disciple, and makes that remark to the Master; the only difference is, that he makes it in the nineteenth instead of the first century.

Is there a choir in Mr. T.'s church? And does it ever occur that they have no better manners than to sing that hymn which is so suggestive of laborers and mechanics:

> Son of the Carpenter! receive
> This humble work of mine?

Now, can it be possible that in a handful of centuries the Christian character has fallen away from an imposing heroism that scorned even the stake, the cross, and the axe, to a poor little effeminacy that withers and wilts under an unsavory smell? We are not prepared to believe so, the reverend Doctor and his friend to the contrary notwithstanding.

Bible Teaching and Religious Practice (1890)

Religion had its share in the changes of civilization and national character, of course. What share? The lion's. In the history of the human race this has always been the case, will always be the case, to the end of time, no doubt; or at least until man by the slow processes of evolution shall develop into something really fine and high—some billions of years hence, say.

The Christian's Bible is a drug store. Its contents remain the same; but the medical practice changes. For eighteen hundred years these changes were slight—scarcely noticeable. The practice was allopathic—allopathic in its rudest and crudest form. The dull and ignorant physician day and night, and all the days and all the nights, drenched his patient with vast and hideous doses of the most repulsive drugs to be found in the store's stock; he bled him, cupped him, purged him, puked him, salivated him, never gave his system a chance to rally, nor nature a chance to help. He kept him religion sick for eighteen centuries, and allowed him not a well day during all that time. The stock in the store was made up of about equal portions of baleful and debilitating poisons, and healing and comforting medicines; but the practice of the time confined the physician to the use of the former; by consequence, he could only damage his patient, and that is what he did.

Not until far within our century was any considerable change in the practice introduced; and then mainly, or in effect only, in Great Britain and the United States. In the other countries to-day, the patient either still takes the ancient treatment or does not call the physician at all. In the English-speaking countries the changes observable in our century were forced by that very thing just referred to—the revolt of the patient against the system; they were not projected by the physician. The patient fell to doctoring himself, and the physician's practice began to fall off. He modified his method to get back his trade. He did it gradually, reluctantly; and never yielded more at a time than the pressure compelled. At first he relinquished the daily dose of hell and damnation, and administered it every other day only; next he allowed another day to pass; then another and presently another; when he had restricted it at last to Sundays, and imagined that now there would surely be a truce, the homoeopath arrived on the field and made him abandon hell and damnation altogether, and administered Christ's love, and comfort, and charity and compassion in its stead. These had been in the drug store all the time, gold labeled and conspicuous among the long shelfloads of repulsive purges and vomits and poisons, and so the practice was to blame that they had remained unused, not the pharmacy. To the ecclesiastical physician of fifty years ago, his predecessor of fifty years ago was a quack. To the every-man-his-own-ecclesiastical-doctor of—when?—what will the ecclesiastical physician of to-day be? Unless evolution, which has been a truth ever since the globes, suns, and planets of the solar system were but wandering films of meteor dust, shall reach a limit and become a lie, there is but one fate in store for him.

The methods of the priest and the parson have been very curious, their history is very entertaining. In all the ages the Roman Church has owned slaves, bought and sold slaves, authorized and encouraged her children to trade in them. Long after some Christian peoples had freed their slaves the Church still held on to hers. If any could know, to absolute certainty, that all this was right, and according to God's will and desire, surely it was she, since she was God's specially appointed representative in the earth and sole authorized infallible expounder of his Bible. There were the texts; there was no mistaking their meaning; she was right, she was doing in this thing what the Bible had mapped out for her to do. So unassailable was her position that in all the centuries she had no word to say against human slavery. Yet now at last, in our immediate day, we hear a Pope saying slave trading is wrong, and we see him sending an expedition to Africa to stop it. The texts remain: it is the practice that has changed. Why? Because the world has corrected the Bible. The Church never corrects it; and also never fails to drop in at the tail of the procession—and take the credit of the correction. As she will presently do in this instance.

Christian England supported slavery and encouraged it for two hundred and fifty years, and her Church's consecrated ministers looked on, sometimes taking an active hand, the rest of the time indifferent. England's interests in the business may be called a Christian interest, a Christian industry. She had her full share in its revival after a long period of inactivity, and this revival was a Christian monopoly; that is to say, it was in the hands of Christian countries exclusively. English parliaments aided the slave traffic and protected it; two English kings held stock in slave-catching companies. The first regular English slave hunter—John Hawkins, of still revered memory—made such successful havoc, on his second voyage, in the matter of surprising and burning villages, and maiming, slaughtering, capturing, and selling their unoffending inhabitants, that his delighted queen conferred the chivalric honor of knighthood on him—a rank which had acquired its chief esteem and distinction in other and earlier fields of Christian effort. The new knight, with characteristic English frankness and brusque simplicity, chose as his device the figure of a negro slave, kneeling and in chains. Sir John's work was the invention of Christians, was to remain a bloody and awful monopoly in the hands of Christians for a quarter of a millennium, was to destroy homes, separate families, enslave friendless men and women, and break a myriad of human hearts, to the end that Christian nations might be prosperous and comfortable, Christian churches be built, and the gospel of the meek and merciful Redeemer be spread abroad in the earth; and so in the name of his ship, unsuspected but eloquent and clear, lay hidden prophecy. She was called *The Jesus*.

But at last in England, an illegitimate Christian rose against slavery. It is curious that when a Christian rises against a rooted wrong at all, he is usually an illegitimate Christian, member of some despised and bastard sect. There was a bitter struggle, but in the end the slave trade had to go—and went. The Biblical authorization remained, but the practice changed.

Then—the usual thing happened; the visiting English critic among us began straightway to hold up his pious hands in horror at our slavery. His distress was unappeasable, his words full of bitterness and contempt. It is true we had not so many as fifteen hundred thousand slaves for him to worry about, while his England still owned twelve millions, in her foreign possessions; but that fact did not modify his wail any, or stay his tears, or soften his censure. The fact that every time we had tried to get rid of our slavery in previous generations, but had always been obstructed, balked, and defeated by England, was a matter of no consequence to him; it was ancient history, and not worth the telling.

Our own conversion came at last. We began to stir against slavery. Hearts grew soft, here, there, and yonder. There was no place in the land where the seeker could not find some small budding sign of pity for the slave. No place in all the land but one—the pulpit. It yielded at last; it always does. It fought a strong and stubborn fight, and then did what it always does, joined the procession—at the tail end. Slavery fell. The slavery text remained; the practice changed, that was all.

During many ages there were witches. The Bible said so. The Bible commanded that they should not be allowed to live. Therefore the Church, after doing its duty in but a lazy and indolent way for eight hundred years, gathered up its halters, thumbscrews, and firebrands and set about its holy work in earnest. She worked hard at it night and day during nine centuries and imprisoned, tortured, hanged, and burned whole hordes and armies of witches, and washed the Christian world clean with their foul blood.

Then it was discovered that there was no such thing as witches, and never had been. One does not know whether to laugh or to cry. Who discovered that there was no such thing as a witch—the priest, the parson? No, these never discover anything. At Salem, the parson clung pathetically to his witch text after the laity had abandoned it in remorse and tears for the crimes and cruelties it had persuaded them to do. The parson wanted more blood, more shame, more brutalities; it was the unconsecrated laity that stayed his hand. In Scotland the parson killed the witch after the magistrate had pronounced her innocent; and when the merciful legislature proposed to sweep the hideous laws against witches from the statute book, it was the parson who came imploring, with tears and imprecations, that they be suffered to stand.

There are no witches. The witch text remains; only the practice has changed. Hell fire is gone, but the text remains. Infant damnation is gone, but the text remains. More than two hundred death penalties are gone from the law books, but the texts that authorized them remain.

Is it not well worthy of note that of all the multitude of texts through which man has driven his annihilating pen he has never once made the mistake of obliterating a good and useful one? It does certainly seem to suggest that if man continues in the direction of enlightenment, his religious practice may, in the end, attain some semblance of human decency.

From *The Adventures of Huckleberry Finn:* "A River Village and a Lynch Mob" (1884)

All the streets and lanes was just mud, they warn't nothing else *but* mud—mud as black as tar, and nigh about a foot deep in some places; and two or three inches deep in *all* the places. The hogs loafed and grunted around, everywheres. You'd see a muddy sow and a litter of pigs come lazying along the street and whollop herself right down in the way, where folks had to walk around her, and she'd stretch out, and shut her eyes, and wave her ears, whilst the pigs was milking her, and look as happy as if she was on salary. And pretty soon you'd hear a loafer sing out, "Hi! *so* boy! sick him, Tige!" and away the sow would go, squealing most horrible, with a dog or two swinging to each ear, and three or four dozen more a-coming; and then you would see all the loafers get up and watch the thing out of sight, and laugh at the fun and look grateful for the noise. Then they'd settle back again till there was a dog-fight. There couldn't anything wake them up all over, and make them happy all over, like a dog-fight—unless it might be putting turpentine on a stray dog and setting fire to him, or tying a tin pan to his tail and see him run himself to death.

On the river front some of the houses was sticking out over the bank, and they was bowed and bent, and about ready to tumble in. The people had moved out of them. The bank was caved away under one corner of some others, and that corner was hanging over. People lived in them yet, but it was dangersome, because sometimes a strip of land as wide as a house caves in at a time. Sometimes a belt of land a quarter of a mile deep will start in and cave along and cave along till it all caves into the river in one summer. Such a town as that has to be always moving back, and back, and back, because the river's always gnawing at it.

The nearer it got to noon that day, the thicker and thicker was the wagons and horses in the streets, and more coming all the time. Families fetched their dinners with them, from the country, and eat them in the wagons. There was considerable whiskey drinking going on, and I seen three fights. By-and-by somebody sings out—

"Here comes old Boggs!—in from the country for his little old monthly drunk—here he comes, boys!"

All the loafers looked glad—I reckoned they was used to having fun out of Boggs. One of them says—

"Wonder who he's a gwyne to chaw up this time. If he'd a chawed up all the men he's been a gwyne to chaw up in the last twenty year, he'd have considerable ruputation, now."

Another one says, "I wisht old Boggs'd threaten me, 'cuz then I'd know I warn't gwyne to die for a thousan' year."

Boggs comes a-tearing along on his horse, whooping and yelling like an Injun, and singing out—

"Cler the track, thar. I'm on the waw-path, and the price uv coffins is a gwyne to raise."

He was drunk, and weaving about in his saddle; he was over fifty year old, and had a very red face.

Everybody yelled at him, and laughed at him, and sassed him, and he sassed back, and said he'd attend to them and lay them out in their regular turns, but he couldn't wait now, because he'd come to town to kill old Colonel Sherburn, and his motto was, "meat first, and spoon vittles to top off on."

He see me, and rode up and says—

"Whar'd you come f'm, boy? You prepared to die?"

Then he rode on. I was scared; but a man says—

"He don't mean nothing; he's always a carryin' on like that, when he's drunk. He's the best-naturedest old fool in Arkansaw—never hurt nobody, drunk nor sober."

Boggs rode up before the biggest store in town and bent his head down so he could see under the curtain of the awning, and yells—

"Come out here, Sherburn! Come out and meet the man you've swindled. You're the houn' I'm after, and I'm a gwyne to have you, too!"

And so he went on, calling Sherburn everything he could lay his tongue to, and the whole street packed with people listening and laughing and going on. By-and-by a proud-looking man about fifty-five—and he was a heap the best dressed man in that town, too—steps out of the store, and the crowd drops back on each side to let him come. He says to Boggs, mighty ca'm and slow—he says:

"I'm tired of this; but I'll endure it till one o'clock. Till one o'clock, mind—no longer. If you open your mouth against me only once, after that time, you can't travel so far but I will find you."

Then he turns and goes in. The crowd looked mighty sober; nobody stirred, and there warn't no more laughing. Boggs rode off blackguarding Sherburn as loud as he could yell, all down the street; and pretty soon back he comes and stops before the store, still keeping it up. Some men crowded around him and tried to get him to shut up, but he wouldn't; they told him it would be one o'clock in about fifteen minutes, and so he *must* go home—he must go right away. But it didn't do no good. He cussed away, with all his might, and throwed his hat down in the mud and rode over it, and pretty soon away he went a-raging down the street again, with his gray hair a-flying. Everybody that could get a chance at him tried their best to coax him off of his horse so they could lock him up and get him sober; but it warn't no use—up the street he would tear again, and give Sherburn another cussing. By-and-by somebody says—

"Go for his daughter!—quick, go for his daughter; sometimes he'll listen to her. If anybody can persuade him, she can."

So somebody started on a run. I walked down street a ways, and stopped. In about five or ten minutes, here comes Boggs again—but not on his horse. He was a-reeling across the street towards me, bareheaded, with a friend on both sides of him aholt of his arms and hurrying him along. He was quiet, and looked uneasy; and he warn't hanging back any, but was doing some of the hurrying himself. Somebody sings out—

"Boggs!"

I looked over there to see who said it, and it was that Colonel Sherburn. He was standing perfectly still, in the street, and had a pistol raised in his right hand—not aiming it, but holding it out with the barrel tilted up towards the sky. The same second I see a young girl coming on the run, and two men with her. Boggs and the men turned round, to see who called him, and when they see the pistol the men jumped to one side, and the pistol barrel come down slow and steady to a level—both barrels cocked. Boggs throws up both of his hands, and says, "O Lord, don't shoot!" Bang! goes the first shot, and he staggers back clawing at the air—bang! goes the second one, and he tumbles backwards onto the ground, heavy and solid, with his arms spread out. That young girl screamed out, and comes rushing, and down she throws herself on her father, crying, and saying, "Oh, he's killed him, he's killed him!" The crowd closed up around them, and shouldered and jammed one another, with their necks stretched, trying to see, and people on the inside trying to shove them back, and shouting, "Back, back! give him air, give him air!"

Colonel Sherburn he tossed his pistol onto the ground, and turned around on his heels and walked off.

They took Boggs to a little drug store, the crowd pressing around, just the same, and the whole town following, and I rushed and got a good place at the window, where I was close to him and could see in. They laid him on the floor, and put one large Bible under his head, and opened another one and spread it on his breast—but they tore open his shirt first, and I seen where one of the bullets went in. He made about a dozen long gasps, his breast lifting the Bible up when he drawed in his breath, and letting it down again when he breathed it out—and after that he laid still; he was dead. Then they pulled his daughter away from him, screaming and crying, and took her off. She was about sixteen, and very sweet and gentle-looking, but awful pale and scared.

Well, pretty soon the whole town was there, squirming and scrouging and pushing and shoving to get at the window and have a look, but people that had the places wouldn't give them up, and folks behind them was saying all the time, "Say, now, you've looked enough, you fellows; 'taint right and 'taint fair, for you to stay thar all the time, and never give nobody a chance; other folks has their rights as well as you."

There was considerable jawing back, so I slid out, thinking maybe there was going to be trouble. The streets was full, and everybody was excited. Everybody that seen the shooting was telling how it happened, and there was a big crowd packed around each one of these fellows, stretching their necks and listening. One long lanky man, with long hair and a big white fur stovepipe hat on the back of his head, and a crooked-handled cane, marked out the places on the ground where Boggs stood, and where Sherburn stood, and the people following him around from one place to t'other and watching everything he done, and bobbing their heads to show they understood, and stooping a little and resting their hands on their thighs to watch him mark the places on the ground with his cane; and then he stood up straight and stiff where Sherburn had stood, frowning and having his hat-brim down over his eyes, and sung out, "Boggs!" and then fetched his cane down slow to a level, and says "Bang!" staggered backwards, says "Bang!" again, and fell down flat on his back. The people that had seen the thing said he done it perfect; said it was just exactly the way it all happened. Then as much as a dozen people got out their bottles and treated him.

Well, by-and-by somebody said Sherburn ought to be lynched. In about a minute everybody was saying it; so way they went, mad and yelling, and snatching down every clothes-line they come to, to do the hanging with.

They swarmed up the street towards Sherburn's house, a-whooping and yelling and raging like Injuns, and everything had to clear the way or get run over and tromped to mush, and it was awful to see. Children was heeling it ahead of the mob, screaming and trying to get out of the way; and every window along the road was full of women's heads, and there was nigger boys in every tree, and bucks and wenches looking over every fence; and as soon as the mob would get nearly to them they would break and skaddle back out of reach. Lots of the women and girls was crying and taking on, scared most to death.

They swarmed up in front of Sherburn's palings as thick as they could jam together, and you couldn't hear yourself think for the noise. It was a little twenty-foot yard. Some sung out "Tear down the fence! tear down the fence!" Then there was a racket of ripping and tearing and smashing, and down she goes, and the front wall of the crowd begins to roll in like a wave.

Just then Sherburn steps out on to the roof of his little front porch, with a double-barrel gun in his hand, and takes his stand, perfectly ca'm and deliberate, not saying a word. The racket stopped, and the wave sucked back.

Sherburn never said a word—just stood there, looking down. The stillness was awful creepy and uncomfortable. Sherburn run his eye slow along the crowd; and wherever it struck, the people tried a little to outgaze him, but they couldn't; they dropped their eyes and looked sneaky. Then pretty soon Sherburn sort of laughed; not the pleasant kind, but the kind that makes you feel like when you are eating bread that's got sand in it.

Then he stays, slow and scornful:

"The idea of *you* lynching anybody! It's amusing. The idea of you thinking you had pluck enough to lynch a *man!* Because you're brave enough to tar and feather poor friendless cast-out women that come along here, did that make you think you had grit enough to lay your hands on a *man?* why, a *man's* safe in the hands of ten thousand of your kind—as long as it's day-time and you're not behind him.

"Do I know you? I know you clear through. I was born and raised in the South, and I've lived in the North; so I know the average all around. The average man's a coward. In the North he lets anybody walk over him that wants to, and goes home and prays for a humble spirit to bear it. In the South one man, all by himself, has stopped a stage full of men, in the day-time, and robbed the lot. Your newspapers call you a brave people so much that you think you *are* braver than any other people—whereas you're just *as* brave, and no braver. Why don't your juries hang murderers? Because they're afraid the man's friends will shoot them in the back, in the dark —and it's just what they *would* do.

"So they always acquit; and then a *man* goes in the night, with a hundred masked cowards at his back, and lynches the rascal. Your mistake is, that you didn't bring a man with you; that's one mistake, and the other is that you didn't come in the dark, and fetch your masks. You brought *part* of a man—Buck Harkness, there—and if you hadn't had him to start you, you'd a taken it out in blowing.

"You didn't want to come. The average man don't like trouble and danger. *You* don't like trouble and danger. But if only *half* a man—like Buck Harkness, there—shouts 'Lynch him, lynch him!' you're afraid to back down—afraid you'll be found out to be what you are—*cowards*—and so you raise a yell, and hang yourselves onto that half-a-man's coat tail, and come raging up here, swearing what big things you're going to do. The pitifulest thing out is a mob; that's what an army is—a mob; they don't fight with courage that's born in them, but with courage that's borrowed from their mass, and from their officers. But a mob without any *man* at the head of it, is *beneath* pitifulness. Now the thing for *you* to do, is to droop your tails and go home and crawl in a hole. If any real lynching's going to be done, it will be done in the dark, southern fashion; and when they come they'll bring their masks, and fetch a *man* along. Now *leave*—and take your half-a-man with you"—tossing his gun up across his left arm and cocking it, when he says this.

The crowd washed back sudden, and then broke all

apart and went tearing off every which way, and Buck Harkness he heeled it after them, looking tolerable cheap. I could a staid, if I'd a wanted to, but I didn't want to.

The United States of Lyncherdom
(1901)

I

And so Missouri has fallen, that great state! Certain of her children have joined the lynchers, and the smirch is upon the rest of us. That handful of her children have given us a character and labeled us with a name, and to the dwellers in the four quarters of the earth we are "lynchers," now, and ever shall be. For the world will not stop and think—it never does, it is not its way; its way is to generalize from a single sample. It will not say, "Those Missourians have been busy eighty years in building an honorable good name for themselves; these hundred lynchers down in the corner of the state are not real Missourians, they are renegades." No, that truth will not enter its mind; it will generalize from the one or two misleading samples and say, "The Missourians are lynchers." It has no reflection, no logic, no sense of proportion. With it, figures go for nothing; to it, figures reveal nothing, it cannot reason upon them rationally; it would say, for instance, that China is being swiftly and surely Christianized, since nine Chinese Christians are being made every day; and it would fail, with him, to notice that the fact that 33,000 pagans are *born* there every day, damages the argument. It would say, "There are a hundred lynchers there, therefore the Missourians are lynchers"; the considerable fact that there are two and a half million Missourians who are *not* lynchers would not affect their verdict.

II

Oh, Missouri!

The tragedy occurred near Pierce City, down in the southwestern corner of the state. On a Sunday afternoon a young white woman who had started alone from church was found murdered. For there are churches there; in my time religion was more general, more pervasive, in the South than it was in the North, and more virile and earnest, too, I think; I have some reason to believe that this is still the case. The young woman was found murdered. Although it was a region of churches and schools the people rose, lynched three negroes—two of them very aged ones—burned out five negro households, and drove thirty negro families into the woods.

I do not dwell upon the provocation which moved the people to these crimes, for that has nothing to do with the matter; the only question is, does the assassin *take the law into his own hands?* It is very simple, and very just. If the assassin be proved to have usurped the law's prerogative in righting his wrongs, that ends the matter; a thousand provocations are no defense. The Pierce City people had bitter provocation—indeed, as revealed by certain of the particulars, the bitterest of all provocations—but no matter, they took the law into their own hands, when by the terms of their statutes their victims would certainly hang if the law had been allowed to take its course, for there are but few negroes in that region and they are without authority and without influence in overawing juries.

Why has lynching, with various barbaric accompaniments, become a favorite regulator in cases of "the usual crime" in several parts of the country? Is it because men think a lurid and terrible punishment a more forcible object lesson and a more effective deterrent than a sober and colorless hanging done privately in a jail would be? Surely sane men do not think that. Even the average child should know better. It should know that any strange and much-talked-of event is always followed by imitations, the world being so well supplied with excitable people who only need a little stirring up to make them lose what is left of their heads and do mad things which they would not have thought of ordinarily. It should know that if a man jump off Brooklyn Bridge another will imitate him; that if a person venture down Niagara Whirlpool in a barrel another will imitate him; that if a Jack the Ripper make notoriety by slaughtering women in dark alleys he will be imitated; that if a man attempt a king's life and the newspapers carry the noise of it around the globe, regicides will crop up all around. The child should know that one much-talked-of outrage and murder committed by a negro will upset the disturbed intellects of several other negroes and produce a series of the very tragedies the community would so strenuously wish to prevent; that each of these crimes will produce another series, and year by year steadily increase the tale of these disasters instead of diminishing it; that, in a word, the lynchers are themselves the worst enemies of their women. The child should also know that by a law of our make, communities, as well as individuals, are imitators; and that a much-talked-of lynching will infallibly produce other lynchings here and there and yonder, and that in time these will breed a mania, a fashion; a fashion which will spread wide and wider, year by year, covering state after state, as with an advancing disease. Lynching has reached Colorado, it has reached California, it has reached Indiana—and now Missouri! I may live to see a negro burned in Union Square, New York, with fifty thousand people present, and not a sheriff visible, not a governor, not a constable, not a colonel, not a clergyman, not a law-and-order representative of any sort.

Increase in Lynching.—In 1900 there were eight more cases than in 1899, and probably this year there will be more than there were last year. The year is little more than half gone, and yet there are eighty-eight cases as compared with one hundred and fifteen for all of last year. The four Southern states, Alabama, Georgia, Louisiana, and Mississippi are the worst offenders. Last year there were eight cases in Alabama, sixteen in Georgia, twenty in Louisiana, and twenty in Mississippi—over one-half the total. This year to date there have been nine in Alabama, twelve in Georgia, eleven in Louisiana, and thirteen in Mississippi—again more than one-half the total number in the whole United States.—Chicago *Tribune.*

It must be that the increase comes of the inborn human instinct to imitate—that and man's commonest weakness, his aversion to being unpleasantly conspicuous, pointed at, shunned, as being on the unpopular side. Its other name is Moral Cowardice, and is the commanding feature of the make-up of 9,999 men in the 10,000. I am not offering this as a discovery; privately the dullest of us knows it to be true. History will not allow us to forget or ignore this supreme trait of our character. It persistently and sardonically reminds us that from the beginning of the world no revolt against a public infamy or oppression has ever been begun but by the one daring man in the 10,000, the rest timidly waiting, and slowly and reluctantly joining, under the influence of that man and his fellows from the other ten thousands. The abolitionists remember. Privately the public feeling was with them early, but each man was afraid to speak out until he got some hint that his neighbor was privately feeling as he privately felt himself. Then the boom followed. It always does. It will occur in New York, some day; and even in Pennsylvania.

It has been supposed—and said—that the people at a lynching enjoy the spectacle and are glad of a chance to see it. It cannot be true; all experience is against it. The people in the South are made like the people in the North—the vast majority of whom are right-hearted and compassionate, and would be cruelly pained by such a spectacle—and *would attend it,* and let on to be pleased with it, if the public approval seemed to require it. We are made like that, and we cannot help it. The other animals are not so, but we cannot help that, either. They lack the Moral Sense; we have no way of trading ours off, for a nickel or some other thing above its value. The Moral Sense teaches us what is right, and how to avoid it —when unpopular.

It is thought, as I have said, that a lynching crowd enjoys a lynching. It certainly is not true; it is impossible of belief. It is freely asserted—you have seen it in print many times of late—that the lynching impulse has been misinterpreted; that it is *not* the outcome of a spirit of revenge, but of a "mere atrocious hunger *to look upon human suffering.*" If that were so, the crowds that saw the Windsor Hotel burn down would have enjoyed the horrors that fell under their eyes. Did they? No one will think that of them, no one will make that charge. Many risked their lives to save the men and women who were in peril. Why did they do that? Because *none would disapprove.* There was no restraint; they could follow their natural impulse. Why does a crowd of the same kind of people in Texas, Colorado, Indiana, stand by, smitten to the heart and miserable, and by ostentatious outward signs pretend to enjoy a lynching? Why does it lift no hand or voice in protest? Only because it would be unpopular to do it, I think; each man is afraid of his neighbor's disapproval—a thing which, to the general run of the race, is more dreaded than wounds and death. When there is to be a lynching the people hitch up and come miles to see it, bringing their wives and children. Really to see it? No—they come only because they are afraid to stay at home, lest it be noticed and offensively commented upon. We may believe this, for we all know how *we* feel about such spectacles—also, how we would act under the like pressure. We are not any better nor any braver than anybody else, and we must not try to creep out of it.

A Savonarola can quell and scatter a mob of lynchers with a mere glance of his eye: so can a Merrill * or a Beloat.† For no mob has any sand in the presence of a man known to be splendidly brave. Besides, a lynching mob would *like* to be scattered, for of a certainty there are never ten men in it who would not prefer to be somewhere else—and would be, if they but had the courage to go. When I was a boy I saw a brave gentleman deride and insult a mob and drive it away; and afterward, in Nevada, I saw a noted desperado make two hundred men sit still, with the house burning under them, until he gave them permission to retire. A plucky man can rob a whole passenger train by himself; and the half of a brave man can hold up a stagecoach and strip its occupants.

Then perhaps the remedy for lynchings comes to this: station a brave man in each affected community to encourage, support, and bring to light the deep disapproval of lynching hidden in the secret places of its heart—for it is there, beyond question. Then those communities will find something better to imitate—of course, being human, they must imitate something. Where shall these brave men be found? That is indeed a difficulty; there are not three hun-

* Sheriff of Carroll County, Georgia. (M.T.)

† Sheriff, Princeton, Indiana. By that formidable power which lies in an established reputation for cold pluck they faced lynching mobs and securely held the field against them. (M.T.)

dred of them in the earth. If merely *physically* brave men would do, then it were easy; they could be furnished by the cargo. When Hobson called for seven volunteers to go with him to what promised to be certain death, four thousand men responded—the whole fleet, in fact. Because *all the world would approve.* They knew that; but if Hobson's project had been charged with the scoffs and jeers of the friends and associates, whose good opinion and approval the sailors valued, he could not have got his seven.

No, upon reflection, the scheme will not work. There are not enough morally brave men in stock. We are out of moral-courage material; we are in a condition of profound poverty. We have those two sheriffs down South who—but never mind, it is not enough to go around; they have to stay and take care of their own communities.

But if we only *could* have three or four more sheriffs of that great breed! Would it help? I think so. For we are all imitators: other brave sheriffs would follow; to be a dauntless sheriff would come to be recognized as the correct and only thing, and the dreaded disapproval would fall to the share of the other kind; courage in this office would become custom, the absence of it a dishonor, just as courage presently replaces the timidity of the new soldier; then the mobs and the lynchings would disappear, and—

However. It can never be done without some starters, and where are we to get the starters? Advertise? Very well, then, let us advertise.

In the meantime, there is another plan. Let us import American missionaries from China, and send them into the lynching field. With 1,511 of them out there converting two Chinamen apiece per annum against an uphill birth rate of 33,000 pagans per day,* it will take upward of a million years to make the conversions balance the output and bring the Christianizing of the country in sight to the naked eye; therefore, if we can offer our missionaries as rich a field at home at lighter expense and quite satisfactory in the matter of danger, why shouldn't they find it fair and right to come back and give us a trial? The Chinese are universally conceded to be excellent people, honest, honorable, industrious, trustworthy, kind-hearted and all that—leave them alone, they are plenty good enough just as they are; and besides, almost every convert runs a risk of catching our civilization. We ought to be careful. We ought to think twice before we encourage a risk like that; for, *once civilized, China can never be uncivilized again.* We have not been thinking of that. Very well, we ought to think of it now. Our missionaries will find that we have a field for them—and not only for the 1,511, but for 15,011. Let them look at the following telegram and see if they have anything in China that is more appetizing. It is from Texas:

> The negro was taken to a tree and swung in the air. Wood and fodder were piled beneath his body and a hot fire was made. *Then it was suggested that the man ought*

* These figures are not fanciful; all of them are genuine and authentic. They are from official missionary records in China. See Doctor Morrison's book on his pedestrian journey across China; he quotes them and gives his authorities. For several years he has been the London *Times*'s representative in Peking, and was there through the siege. (M.T.)

not to die too quickly, and he was let down to the ground while a party went to Dexter, about two miles distant, to procure coal oil. This was thrown on the flames and the work completed.

We implore them to come back and help us in our need. Patriotism imposes this duty on them. Our country is worse off than China; they are our countrymen, their motherland supplicates their aid in this her hour of deep distress. They are competent; our people are not. They are used to scoffs, sneers, revilings, danger; our people are not. They have the martyr spirit; nothing but the martyr spirit can brave a lynching mob, and cow it and scatter it. They can save their country, we beseech them to come home and do it. We ask them to read that telegram again, and yet again, and picture the scene in their minds, and soberly ponder it; then multiply it by 115, add 88; place the 203 in a row, allowing 600 feet of space for each human torch, so that there may be viewing room around it for 5,000 Christian American men, women, and children, youths and maidens; make it night, for grim effect; have the show in a gradually rising plain, and let the course of the stakes be uphill; the eye can then take in the whole line of twenty-four miles of blood-and-flesh bonfires unbroken, whereas if it occupied level ground the ends of the line would bend down and be hidden from view by the curvature of the earth. All being ready, now, and the darkness opaque, the stillness impressive—for there should be no sound but the soft moaning of the night wind and the muffled sobbing of the sacrifices—let all the far stretch of kerosened pyres be touched off simultaneously and the glare and the shrieks and the agonies burst heavenward to the Throne.

There are more than a million persons present; the light from the fires flushes into vague outline against the night the spires of five thousand churches. O kind missionary, O compassionate missionary, leave China! Come home and convert these Christians!

I believe that if anything can stop this epidemic of bloody insanities it is martial personalities that can face mobs without flinching; and as such personalities are developed only by familiarity with danger and by the training and seasoning which come of resisting it, the likeliest place to find them must be among the missionaries who have been under tuition in China during the past year or two. We have abundance of work for them, and for hundreds and thousands more, and the field is daily growing and spreading. Shall we find them? We can try. In 75,000,000 there must be other Merrills and Beloats; and it is the law of our make that each example shall wake up drowsing chevaliers of the same great knighthood and bring them to the front.

Letter to Jules Hart
(1901)

Evidently written in reply to a personal request from Hart, which is not in the files of the Mark Twain Papers, Mark Twain's letter was followed by a cautionary note: "If you use my yesterday's letter, please erase the last two words. . . . Also please erase the inverted commas which enclose the word 'Civilization.' . . .*

"With these coarsenesses expunged the letter will be decent enough."

Dear Sir:

When politics enter into municipal government, nothing resulting therefrom in the way of crimes and infamies is then incredible. It actually enables one to accept and believe the impossible: for instance, your statement that the death-rate at the slaughter-house on Blackwell's Island called the Infant's "Home" is 900 in the thousand! In God's name why do they not bury those poor little creatures as soon as they are received in that hospitable hell, and so save them some part of their sufferings? During the past three days we have been standing aghast at the death-rate in the British concentration-camps in South Africa—250 in the thousand (children, mainly)—and now

* As is evident in the letter Mark Twain meant the last four words. (F.A.)

you come with this death-rate, which makes that one look wholesome, healthy, robust!

What do they feed our little concentrados on, in that Blackwell's Island Cemetery? Prussic acid and exposure? Can anything else account for such a death-rate?—a death-rate which exceeds the death-rate of any war that was ever fought, of any famine or any pestilence that has ever visited the earth, and can even laugh to scorn the death-rate of the supremest of *all* historical death-rates, that of the monumental disaster of the Black Hole of Calcutta!

And now you tell me—in contrast with this devilish showing—that the death-rate in your Hebrew Infant Asylum is only 40 in the thousand! Oh, be good, be kind, be generous—take our little Christians in there, and save them from the bitter misery and temporal damnation of governmental Christian charity! Oh, save their lives, and send them missionarying to China to spread our darling "Civilization," which we think so much of. When we are drunk.

Truly yours,
MARK TWAIN

Extract from Article in "'The Radical,' Jan., 916" (1906?)

This fragment dated 916, as given here, or 1906, by simple transposition of numbers, the year in which it was most likely written, expresses its author's evident conviction that the world was over-populated within a few centuries after it was created. The much-revised manuscript begins with a brief "Passage from Eve's Diary" which Mark Twain headed "To follow Abel's death" as part of a chaotic series of diaries and memoirs Mark Twain returned to intermittently throughout much of his life and which he attributed to various members of the "Adam family." After some prefatory remarks in which Eve deplores the fact that "our race now numbers billions," the "extract" begins and incorporates several pages originally written from Eve's point of view. It is evident that Mark Twain had intended to return to the manuscript, possibly to free "The Radical" article entirely from the context of Eve's diary, but even in its present rather elliptical form the piece expresses its author's convictions about a problem that would not attract general concern for well over half a century after his death.*

. . . When the population reached five billions the earth was heavily burdened to support it. But wars, pestilences and famines brought relief, from time to time, and in some degree reduced the prodigious pressure. The memorable benefaction of the year 608, which was a famine reinforced by a pestilence, swept away sixteen hundred millions of people in nine months.

It was not much, but it was something. The same is all that can be said of its successors of later periods. The burden of population grew heavier and heavier and more and more formidable, century by century, and the gravity of the situation created by it was steadily and proportionately increased.

After the age of infancy, few died. The average of life was 600 years. The cradles were filling, filling, filling—always, always, always; the cemeteries stood comparatively idle, the undertakers had but little traffic, they could hardly support their families. The death-rate was 45 in the 1,000,000. To the thoughtful this was portentous; to the light-witted it was matter for brag! These latter were always comparing the population of one decade with that of the previous one and hurrahing over the mighty increase—as if that were an advantage to the world; a world that could hardly scratch enough out of the earth to keep itself from starving.

And yet, worse was to come! Necessarily our true hope did not and could not lie in spasmodic famine and pestilence, whose effects could be only temporary, but in war and the physicians, whose help is constant. Now, then, let us note what has been happening. In the past fifty years science has reduced the doctor's effectiveness by half. He uses but one deadly drug now, where formerly he used ten. Improved sanitation has made whole regions healthy which were previously not so. It has been discovered that the majority of the most useful and fatal diseases are caused by microbes of various breeds; very well, they have learned how to render the efforts of those microbes innocuous. As a result, yellow fever, black plague, cholera, diphtheria, and nearly every valuable distemper we had are become but entertainments for the idle hour, and are of no more value to the State than is the stomach-ache. Marvelous advances in surgery have been added to our disasters. They remove a diseased stomach, now, and the man gets along better and cheaper than he did before. If a man loses a faculty, they bore into his skull and restore it. They take off his legs and arms, and refurnish him from the mechanical junk-shop, and he is as good as new. They give him a new nose if he needs it; new entrails; new bones; new teeth; glass eyes; silver tubes to swallow through; in a word, they take him to pieces and make him over again, and he can stand twice as much wear and tear as he could before. They do these things by help of antiseptics and anaesthesia, and there is no gangrene and no pain. Thus war has become nearly valueless; out of a hundred wounded that would formerly have died, ninety-nine are back in the ranks again in a month.

What, then, is the grand result of all this microbing and sanitation and surgery? This—which is appalling: the death-rate has been reduced to *twenty-two in the million.* And foolish people rejoice at it and boast about it! It is a serious matter. It promises to double the globe's population every twelve months. In time there will not be room in the world for the people to stand, let alone sit down.

Remedy? I know of none. The span of life is too

long, the death-rate is too trifling. The span should be 35 years—a mere moment of time—the death-rate should be 20 or 30 in the *thousand,* not million. Even then the population would double in 35 years, and by and by even this would be a burden again and make the support of life difficult.

Honor to whom honor is due: the physician failed us, war has saved us. Not that the killed and wounded amount to anything as a relief, for they do not; but the poverty and desolation caused by war sweep myriads away and make space for immigrants. War is a rude friend, but a kind one. It keeps us down to 60,000,000,000 and saves the hard-grubbing world alive. It is all that the globe can support. . . .

The Dervish and the Offensive Stranger (1902)

The Dervish: I will say again, and yet again, and still again, that a good deed—

The Offensive Stranger: Peace, oh man of narrow vision! There is no such thing as a good *deed*—

The Dervish: O shameless blasphe—

The Offensive Stranger: And no such thing as an evil deed. There are good *impulses*, there are evil impulses, and that is all. Half of the results of a good intention are evil; half the results of an evil intention are good. No man can command the results, nor allot them.

The Dervish: And so—

The Offensive Stranger: And so you shall praise men for their good intentions, and not blame them for the evils resulting; you shall blame men for their evil intentions, and not praise them for the good resulting.

The Dervish: O, maniac! will you say—

The Offensive Stranger: Listen to the law: From *every* impulse, whether good or evil, flows two streams; the one carries health, the other carries poison. From the beginning of time this law has not changed, to the end of time it will not change.

The Dervish: If I should strike thee dead in anger—

The Offensive Stranger: Or kill me with a drug

which you hoped would give me new life and strength—

The Dervish: Very well. Go on.

The Offensive Stranger: In either case the results would be the same. Age-long misery of mind for you —an evil result; peace, repose, the end of sorrow for me—a good result. Three hearts that hold me dear would break; three pauper cousins of the third remove would get my riches and rejoice; you would go to prison and your friends would grieve, but your humble apprentice-priest would step into your shoes and your fat sleek life and be happy. And are these all the goods and all the evils that would flow from the well-intended or ill-intended act that cut short my life? Oh thoughtless one, Oh purblind creature! the good and evil results that flow from *any* act, even the smallest, breed on and on, century after century, forever and ever and ever, creeping by inches around the globe, affecting all its coming and going populations until the end of time, until the final cataclysm!

The Dervish: Then, there being no such thing as a good deed—

The Offensive Stranger: Don't I tell you there are good *intentions,* and evil ones, and there an end? The *results* are not foreseeable. They are of both kinds, in all cases. It is the law. Listen: this is far-western history:

VOICES OUT OF UTAH

I

The White Chief (to his people): This wide plain was a desert. By our heaven-blest industry we have dammed the river and utilized its waters and turned the desert into smiling fields whose fruitage makes prosperous and happy a thousand homes where poverty and hunger dwelt before. How noble, how beneficent, is Civilization!

II

Indian Chief (to his people): This wide plain, which the Spanish priests taught our fathers to irrigate, was a smiling field, whose fruitage made our homes prosperous and happy. The white American has dammed our river, taken away our water for his own valley, and turned our field into a desert; wherefore we starve.

The Dervish: I perceive that the good intention did really bring both good and evil results in equal measure. But a single case cannot prove the rule. Try again.

The Offensive Stranger: Pardon me, *all* cases prove it. Columbus discovered a new world and gave to the plodding poor and the landless of Europe farms and breathing-space and plenty and happiness—

The Dervish: A good result—

The Offensive Stranger: And they hunted and harried the original owners of the soil, and robbed them, beggared them, drove them from their homes, and exterminated them, root and branch.

The Dervish: An evil result, yes.

The Offensive Stranger: The French Revolution brought desolation to the hearts and homes of five million families and drenched the country with blood and turned its wealth to poverty.

The Dervish: An evil result.

The Offensive Stranger: But every great and precious liberty enjoyed by the nations of Continental Europe to-day are the gift of that Revolution.

The Dervish: A good result, I concede it.

The Offensive Stranger: Is our well-meant effort to lift up the Filipino to our own moral altitude with a musket, we have slipped on the ice and fallen down to his.

The Dervish: A large evil result.

The Offensive Stranger: But as an offset we are a World Power.

The Dervish: Give me time. I must think this one over. Pass on.

The Offensive Stranger: By help of three hundred thousand soldiers and eight hundred million dollars England has succeeded in her good purpose of lifting up the unwilling Boers and making them better and purer and happier than they could ever have become by their own devices.

The Dervish: Certainly that is a good result.

The Offensive Stranger: But there are only eleven Boers left, now.

The Dervish: It has the appearance of an evil result. But I will think it over before I decide.

The Offensive Stranger: Take yet one more instance. With the best intentions the missionary has been laboring in China for eighty years.

The Dervish: The evil result is—

The Offensive Stranger: That nearly a hundred

thousand Chinamen have acquired our Civilization.

The Dervish: And the good result is—

The Offensive Stranger: That by the compassion of God four hundred millions have escaped it.

The Dervish: Adieu, good sir; I am convinced, and accept your Law.

Afterword: The Whole Human Race (1907)

I have not read Nietzsche or Ibsen, nor any other philosopher, and have not needed to do it, and have not desired to do it; I have gone to the fountainhead for information—that is to say, to the human race. Every man is in his own person the whole human race, with not a detail lacking. I am the whole human race without a detail lacking; I have studied the human race with diligence and strong interest all these years in my own person; in myself I find in big or little proportion every quality and every defect that is findable in the mass of the race. I knew I should not find in any philosophy a single thought which had not passed through my own head, nor a single thought which had not passed through the heads of millions and millions of men before I was born; I knew I should not find a single original thought in any philosophy, and I knew I could not furnish one to the world myself, if I had five centuries to invent it in. Nietzsche published his book, and was at once pronounced crazy by the world—by a world which included tens of thousands of bright, sane men who believed exactly as Nietzsche believed, but concealed the fact, and scoffed at Nietzsche. What a coward every man is! and how surely he will find it out if he will just let other people alone and sit down and examine himself. The human race is a race of cowards; and I am not only marching in that procession but carrying a banner.

Editor's Notes

On War

Battle Hymn of the Republic (Brought Down to Date)

The text for this rarely printed piece, written about 1900, is taken from a manuscript in the Mark Twain Papers. Mark Twain probably withheld the parody of Julia Ward Howe's "hymn," whose patriotic purpose he reversed, out of respect for the original author and perhaps because he found no appropriate occasion to publish the piece. The reference, however discreet it may seem, to government-authorized prostitution may also have aroused Mark Twain's apprehension in seeking publication.

The Private History of a Campaign That Failed

The lighthearted account of a Tom Sawyer-like band embarking on an adventure with which this memoir opens darkens into the reality of misery and death which led Mark Twain to flee from involvement in the Civil War and which established his enduring opposition to war. These reminiscences were published in December 1885 in the *Century* magazine in a long series entitled "Battles and Leaders of the Civil War."

As Regards Patriotism

While Mark Twain wrote this, along with many other statements critical of American policies, about 1900, "As Regards Patriotism" was withheld from publication until 1923 when it appeared in *Europe and Elsewhere.* That text was revised and the one given here presents the manuscript as Mark Twain wrote it except that Mark Twain's cancellations have been left out and his characteristic ampersand has been expanded to "and."

Passage from "Glances at History" (Suppressed) Date, 9th Century

As explained in the headnote, "Glances at History" was an imaginary work. Mark Twain's sketch was written about 1906, but not printed until Bernard DeVoto's edition of *Letters from the Earth* appeared in 1962.

From *Mark Twain's Mysterious Stranger Manuscripts: "The Chronicle of Young Satan"*

History of War and Dishonorable War

Although the section of the "Mysterious Stranger" manuscripts from which these excerpts were taken was written in 1900 in direct response to military aggression in South Africa, China, and the Philippines, references to these struggles were ironically eliminated when *The Mysterious Stranger* was published (in a drastically edited version) in 1916. Mark Twain's original texts were first printed in full in

1969 in *Mark Twain's Mysterious Stranger Manuscripts,* edited by William M. Gibson and published by the University of California Press.

Letter to Sylvester Baxter

This letter was first published in *Mark Twain's Letters,* edited by Albert Bigelow Paine in 1917. The present text corrects minor errors in the first printing and appends a postscript missing from the earlier version. In his reply Baxter assured Mark Twain, "I will work in the 'plagiarism,' all right."

Letter to the Editor of Free Russia

Mark Twain's thirteen-page letter on the stationery of the "Onteora Club" where the Clements family stayed in July and August 1890 was never mailed. The envelope is addressed to "Mr. L. Goldenberg, 353 East 83^{d} St, New York City," but no copy of his letter soliciting Mark Twain's views has been found.

Letter to William T. Stead

The February 1890 issue of *The Review of Reviews* contained a thirteen-page article with long quotations on "Mark Twain's New Book," *A Connecticut Yankee,* but the letter to Stead on disarmament was not printed. The first contribution by Mark Twain printed in that journal appeared in the May issue, a 17 March letter addressed to "My Dear Mr. Stead." In the letter, reproduced in facsimile, Mark Twain thanked Stead "for giving my Yankee such a handsome amount of space" and comments on the effectiveness of magazines which allow readers "some swift way of getting at their nuggets without having to pan out their whole mass."

To the Person Sitting in Darkness

In February 1901 the *North American Review* printed Mark Twain's ironic defense of the benefits of a civilization dedicated to war and the exploitation of natives of other lands by American missionaries. Divergent reactions were expressed intensely and passionately in print and in the large number of letters received by Mark Twain. Newspaper response ranged from the New York *Suns*'s:

> We are sorry to say that Mark is on a spree. Don't mention it. For the moment he is in a state of mortifying intoxication from an overdraught of seriousness, something to which his head has not been hardened. Wait, and welcome the prodigal as of old on his return. He will be along again in time.

to the Troy (N.Y.) *Press*'s:

> Mark Twain's masterful paper in the North American Review, "To a Person Sitting in Darkness," should be read by every American. It is able, discriminating, patriotic, effective and enlightening, and breathes the spirit of a true Americanism.

Grief and Mourning for the Night

Mark Twain's anger at a government which misrepresented its massacre of unarmed natives found immediate expression in his "Autobiographical Dictations" of the twelfth and fourteenth of March 1906.

His reminiscences about "schoolmates of sixty years ago" were interrupted by "this incident [which] burst upon the world last Friday." His scornful reaction to the inexplicable slaughter was dictated to his stenographer as the newspaper accounts came in and was collected in *Mark Twain's Autobiography* in 1924.

The War-Prayer

Albert Bigelow Paine first printed extracts from "The War-Prayer" in his 1912 *Biography* of Mark Twain with the comment that the author said he had been urged not to publish it. According to Paine, Mark Twain acceded to its suppression by stating, "I have told the whole truth in that, and only dead men can tell the truth in this world. It can be published after I am dead." A full text was collected in *Europe and Elsewhere* (1923) and now appears in a copy prepared from the typescript bearing Mark Twain's final revisions.

The Human Condition

The Great Revolution in Pitcairn

While Mark Twain was struggling to complete *A Tramp Abroad* he submitted this piece, which he was contemplating as a chapter of the longer work, to the *Atlantic* where it was published in March 1879. "The Great Revolution in Pitcairn" was not included in the account of European travels—apparently it appeared too remote for even that extravagantly structured volume—and was first collected in *The Stolen White Elephant* in 1882.

Goldsmith's Friend Abroad Again

Beyond the allusion to their author these letters have no sustained relationship to *The Citizen of the World.* As the piece progresses and Mark Twain's anger amounts any early attempts at the manner of Goldsmith's irony or even at maintaining an immigrant's point of view diminish. The series of letters was first published in the October and November 1870 issues of the *Galaxy* but was curiously never included in any of Mark Twain's collections of his shorter writings nor in the posthumous "Definitive Edition" of *The Works of Mark Twain.*

A True Story, Repeated Word for Word as I Heard It

The *Atlantic Monthly's* November 1874 publication of Mark Twain's retelling of a family servant's account of her Civil War experiences was Mark Twain's first appearance in the major literary journal of the period. The deceptively simple, almost sentimental, tale does not mask the bitter account of the cruelties of slavery and war and the grief of separation which give substance to the poignant characterization of the narrator.

About Smells

Like "Goldsmith's Friend Abroad Again," this attack on un-Christian class prejudice was written for the *Galaxy* where it was published in May 1870. Neither piece re-emerges in subsequent authorized collections.

Bible Teaching and Religious Practice

Religious hypocrisy and human exploitation formed irresistible targets for Mark Twain's stern reprimand to Christian malpractice. Albert Bigelow Paine noted on the manuscript that it was written in 1890 and completed the last sentence, from the word "continues," in his own handwriting. Paine published it for the first time in *Europe and Elsewhere* in 1923.

From *The Adventures of Huckleberry Finn:* "A River Village and a Lynch Mob"

In 1882 Mark Twain revisited the Mississippi by steamboat from St. Louis to New Orleans. The romance and glory he had experienced as a pilot were largely gone and an impoverished economy and spirit were to be found everywhere. This discovery went into both *Life on the Mississippi* (1883) and *The Adventures of Huckleberry Finn* (1884). The town's mud and the crowd's cowardice provided the themes for this extract from chapters 21 and 22 of the later book.

The United States of Lyncherdom

Before Paine published Mark Twain's attack on the lynching mob, and somewhat less direct attack on American missionaries, in *Europe and Elsewhere*, he removed references to the Reverend Judson Smith, secretary of the American Board of Commissioners for Foreign Missions in 1901, when this piece was written. In the early months of that year Mark Twain and Smith had each contributed two articles about the American missionary to the *North American Re-*

view. One of Mark Twain's was "To the Person Sitting in Darkness." The present manuscript, dated "August 21." by Mark Twain, may have been intended as a further contribution to the controversy.

Letter to Jules Hart

Although Mark Twain gave permission for publication of an edited version of this letter, its previous printing has not been discovered.

Extract from Article in "The Radical," Jan., 916

Like "Glances at History," "The Radical" was an imaginary publication—a conceit which appealed to Mark Twain in 1906. *Letters from the Earth* (1962) was the first publication of both pieces.

The Dervish and the Offensive Stranger

The form of a dialogue to which Mark Twain turned for some of his later polemics usually inspired indifferent results. Here, however, it succinctly brings together so large a number of his opinions that it is surprising he did not publish the conversation, which was first printed in *Europe and Elsewhere* (1923). That text has been corrected against the manuscript in the Mark Twain Papers.

Afterword: *The Whole Human Race*

Mark Twain concluded the daily dictation for his "Autobiography" with this passage on 4 September 1907. The references to Nietzsche and Ibsen derive from a letter written by Archibald Henderson on 26 August 1907 in which he compared Mark Twain's *What Is Man?* to doctrines professed by those writers and by George Bernard Shaw in *The Devil's Disciple.* Mark Twain's identification of himself as foremost among the cowards of the human race is in large measure refuted by his willingness to speak as often and as openly as he did, not only in some of the lesser-known pieces printed in this volume but in the major books in which his reputation is founded.